WINDOWS AND MIRRORS

REFLECTIONS AND TEACHINGS ON CROSS-CULTURAL UNDERSTANDING

DEAN J FUSTO

CONTENTS

ACKNOWLEDGMENTS

When you drink the water…remember the spring

CHINESE PROVERB

I have been gifted with numerous, trajectory-shifting, cross-cultural experiences. My homestays in Spain stand out as foundational experiences in living a culture from the inside-out while the National Endowment for the Humanities Fellowship immersed me in Caribbean culture. My invitations to serve on delegations to St. Lucia, Hong Kong, and Shenzhen enlarged my perspectives in how business is shaped by cultural norms and practices. My two decades (and counting) as an international boarding school leader took me around the world from Vietnam to the Ivory Coast. It was my twenty-year relationship with a family of orphanages throughout the Dominican Republic, however, that truly brought the most profound learning and immersion in what Edward Hall called "deep culture." Joe Barrett and Chris Shepard introduced me to field work in the Dominican Republic, and I am blessed to have known the Diaz family across generations of their leadership and care for hundreds of forgotten and disenfranchised children. Moreover, I remember lovingly the hundreds of faculty and students who traveled alongside me to better understand orphanage life. Our nightly circle reflections beneath moonlit skies were imbued with honest expressions and admissions of privilege, guilt, sadness, joy, and often a hopelessness that births positive action.

Fulfillment, in any career, especially teaching and leading schools, is dependent upon galvanized collaboration and the mission-driven mindset of colleagues. I am forever grateful to the mentors who saw in me the spark of leadership, the seed of promise, and a heart that has guided me to such a joyful life across the continuum of schools I have called home. SIT Graduate Institute rocked my world and challenged every preconceived notion I had regarding the pedagogy of language and culture while deep dives into Dewey at Columbia University furthered my thinking on experiential dimensions of progressive education. In recent years, social impact has been my muse and inspired the founding teachlearn-lead.net, the Center for Global Youth Leadership and Social Entrepreneurial Studies, and TLL Global. I'm grateful to the legions of friends, colleagues, community partners, and students who helped shape my work.

My parents, Mario and Chickie, whose 50 years of devotion to our family restaurant demonstrated how acorns become oak trees and passion for one's work can be sustained over a lifetime. I learned life's greatest lessons (alongside my sister Kim and brother Gregg) washing dishes, being humbled by pig swill, navigating customer idiosyncrasies, enduring the fiscal ebbs and flows of business, and experiencing the afterglow of a hard day's work. My wife, Minh Nguyet, and her family's refugee story profoundly influenced me. I am indebted to her for having embraced my educational nomad lifestyle and insatiable professional wanderlust. In my mother-in-law, Minh Lien, I had an exemplar of one whose life was a love story with the written word. Her obsession with writing elegiac poetry of her war-torn homeland earned her the name "Lady Vietnam." My father-in-law, Dang Khoa, and the grace and humility with which he fully lived life his 103 years.

Finally, at the core of everything I do is my daughter Angelina. At one level, this book is about understanding cultures, amplifying one's window to the world, and learning experientially. At a deeper level, however, the underlying intent of every activity is to facilitate deeper understanding and empathy for other cultures, perspectives, and worldviews. My unwavering hope is that the world Angelina and her children inhabit will be a more peaceful and compassionate one. I am blessed in more ways than could ever be highlighted in the pages of this book. As the Chinese proverb states, I have drunk my share of the water and this book is my way of "remembering the spring."

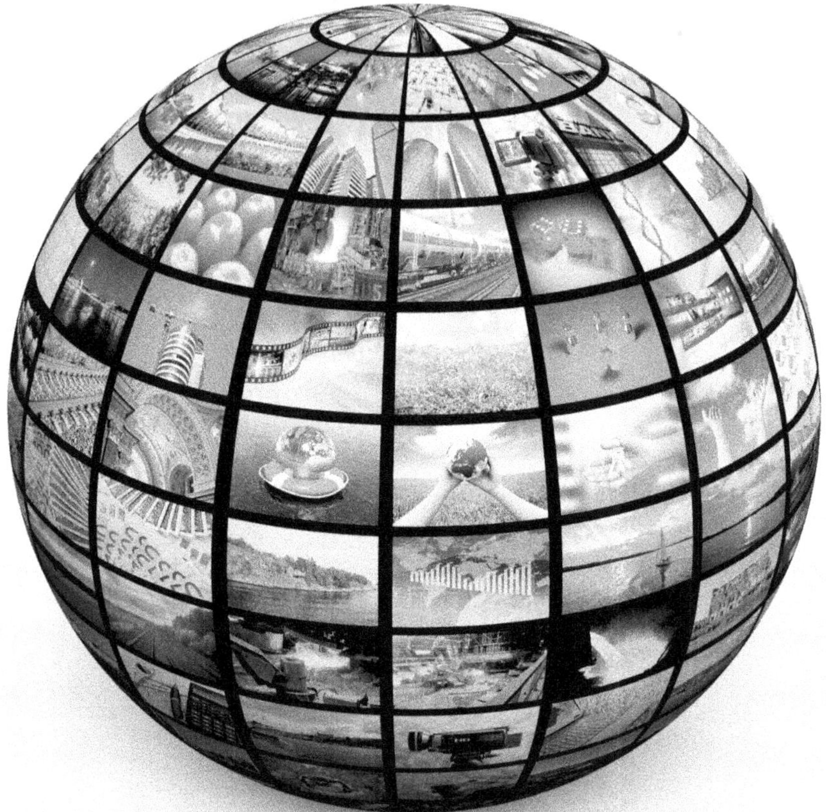

CHAPTER 1
WINDOWS AND MIRRORS

"Sol, sombra, or sol y sombra?" asked my host family. This was likely my first and last bullfight, so I wanted to make a wise choice. On this, the most sweltering day of my college homestay, it seemed most logical to choose shade. That option quickly faded when I learned the price for full sun "sol" was a fraction of the cost for shade. "So, why is there a third option? What is sol y sombra?" I asked. "How can you have both sun and shade in the same instant?" I added. My homestay family giggled and explained, "Sol y sombra is the option that allows you to start the event in full sun, but gradually enjoy the late day shade."

On my first trip to Spain, I was so full of curiosity and questions. The bull fight was one of those moments when I had to put aside my own judgments and preconceived notions and just take it in for what it was. The killing of the bull was not as I had imagined from the textbooks back home in the United States. I had an image of one matador vs. one bull, but I learned that the bull faces many more adversaries than a sole torero. I remember, too, hearing debates in my homestay family about the future of bullfighting and how many in the younger generations of Spain were boycotting

1

this tradition. I remember my own fascination with the topic, but also a reticence to speak up about a deeply held tradition that I knew very little about.

These seminal moments typify the endless discoveries one stumbles upon when traveling or experiencing any culture. In the early 20th century, the notion of culture shock (Lysgaard, S. (1955) became widely heralded and the term has certainly become part of our vernacular to describe any event that outrages, shocks, or mystifies a traveler in a country different from one's own. The reality, however, is that Lysgaard's simplistic views of cultural experiences were too limiting and deterministic. My hope, in this book, is to celebrate each of our more qualitative and human responses to culture and to advance a "seek to understand" mindset toward behaviors, norms, practices, languages, and customs that are different than our own.

Consider for a moment the endless discoveries one stumbles upon when experiencing the culture of another land, the sounds and tones of an unfamiliar tongue, and the perspectives gleaned from seeing the world through another pair of eyes. If we can frame the way we experience and live in the world as a perfect complement of windows and mirrors, our perceptions would be enriched. The cover image for this book captures this highly abstract concept so well. Windows are manufactured in various shapes, sizes, colors, and degrees of heft. Some are fragile while others in the tropics may be engineered to withstand hurricane force winds. There are windows that are blemished with smudges while their stained-glass church counterparts may be considered high art. Finally, there are windows so paper thin that you can hear a symphony of crickets from a faraway field and others built for the big city to be a buffer against ambulance sirens and taxi horns.

If we think of windows as ways to look at or through life itself and cultures specifically, it reminds us of the myriad ways in which we can observe behaviors, norms, practices, and customs. The windows into a culture are always limited by the onlooker as what we see is relegated and shaped by the vantage point we have. When developing cultural awareness, it is healthy and beneficial to move from one window to another i.e., one way of seeing to a different way of seeing. It is also good to remind ourselves that the window we choose is like the attitude we adopt, or the world view we espouse. Windows also give us an outside looking in view or an inside looking out view depending on circumstance.

A mirror is a metacognitive marker for us as we study cultures and develop an awareness of others. It beckons us to look at ourselves in whatever light we choose and demands some reflection. Whereas the window has given us insight into some other place or person, the mirror is all about self and our own image. In the case of crossing-cultures, the mirror could be a journal in which we jot down our thoughts, questions, observations, and interpretations. The mirror can also be a reminder of the change we wish to see in ourselves as we move through the world and challenge ourselves to learn. Finally, a mirror can re-center us after a tough day or challenging events that disrupt our equilibrium.

As we move through this book and its many activities and trainings, the windows and mirrors imagery can be helpful tools for us to frame what we see, experience, and optimize learning and understanding. The first two activities here in chapter one present great ways to build schema and warm-up your students or participants. Before moving forward, take any event from your life today and see it initially for what it is and with the immediate interpretation and response you gave it. Next, look at that same event through an imaginary window with the size, shape, color of your choosing. What, if anything, has changed as you move from window to window? What, if any, value does such a shifting of vantage points and visibility offer you?

HOW TO USE THIS BOOK

Windows and Mirrors: Reflections and Teachings on Cross-Cultural Understanding is intended to be a guide for a broad audience of curious seekers. While most activities were written for teachers and trainers, and used in classroom sessions and curriculum, they have also been a source for sole travelers or small groups who wish to reflect on their experiences of new cultures in novel ways. Based on my thirty years in education and traveling around the globe, I realize how much I think of my own experiences through a teacher's eyes and heart. Thus, the activities and experiences within all have a formulaic structure as if they were mini lessons.

Everything in the book is easily adapted to whatever needs you have or audience you are addressing. I have had families use these activities to connect with each other and enrich shared travel experience. At the same time, I have heard from countless classroom teachers or cross-cultural trainers who use the book to explore different themes and topics with their students. There are instances where I have used the activities as points of departure for my own journaling or reflection. Try not to limit the message of any of the potential teachings and insights by boxing up the contents as labeling it "for teachers only" or "for teens only."

For ease of use and continuity, each activity includes the following structure:

1. Staging
2. Goals
3. Suggested Steps

"Staging" includes ways to set up a venue or learning space to optimize the experience and outcome. It also contains suggestions for special materials or props. Goals refers to what one might extract from participating. I will caution you here that "goals" are solely meant to provide a general outcome but should not be used to limit the possibilities of where an activity could lead. Similar to traveling, you never really know what you might encounter on any adventure. Finally, "Suggested Steps" are a simple succession of ways you can proceed with the activity or experience. They range from being very specific and precise to more open-ended as they are ultimately just suggestions similar to the travel guide that recommends a certain dining spot.

Likewise, the post-activities are expressed in a "Windows and Mirrors" format as you see below.

WINDOWS AND MIRRORS FOLLOW-UP

This section delivers some closing questions to chew on and consider either in conversation with others or in personal journal prompts. Again, as you glance through the 30 plus activities and experiences, be mindful of how you may want to use them. Here are a few suggestions to enhance your reading and the potential insights you glean.

- If you are traveling, use an activity that fits your reflections and prompts you to look at something differently.
- If you are a teacher, consider how your class could benefit from some training or schema building before you engage them in a related lesson. Adapt the content for the age group or subject matter as you see fit.
- If you are a cross-cultural trainer, consider what you currently use to prepare others for their experiences working overseas and use these activities to supplement.
- If you are involved with Diversity, Equity, Inclusion, and Belonging (DEIB) work in schools or other organizations, adapt these activities to what you have designed.
- If you are a guidance counselor or advisor in schools, consider these activities your ally in helping students to

learn skills like empathy, cultural awareness, and the disarming of deleterious stereotypes.
- If your work includes working with newly resettled immigrants or refugees, consider the activities in this book as ways to help them better understand cultural nuances and customs.
- If you are a trip-leader, boost your orientations with the activities found throughout the book but especially in the chapter on service-learning

Treat this book as you would a journey. There are so many ways to deepen and amplify our experience of life and each other. I have reached the five-decade part of life's path and my idealism is still intact. I don't apologize for the assumption I make throughout this book that life is inherently a gift and that we have an obligation to self and each other to be people of empathy with an insatiable hunger to learn. I meet so many folks who truly believe that what they do makes a difference and that our world can be a harmonious one. This book is simply one wave in that ocean.

ACTIVITY 1: WINDOWS AND MIRRORS – FRAMING PERCEPTIONS

Staging: Prepare a space and seating arrangement that maximizes interaction. If possible, choose a venue with many windows. A physical whiteboard or digital screen works best so that you create a "permanent" log of all responses. A supply of sticky notes, pens, markers. Create a slide deck with a varied collection (the wackier, the better) of digital images of windows and mirrors.

Goals: Mastering the Windows and Mirrors framework for cross-cultural awareness and understanding. Build a helpful framework through which one can articulate experiences of other cultures.

Suggested Steps:

1. Explain to everyone that they will be constructing a helpful framework for understanding other cultures and provide some context for the "Windows and Mirrors" mindset that was outlined in the previous pages.

2. Ask participants to use yellow sticky notes to write down a type of window they have seen in their lifetime and to use the green sticky notes to jot down a type of mirror that they have seen or used at any point in their life. They are free to draw an accompanying image of any window or mirror.

3. Answers will vary and capture the different life experiences of all participants.

4. When completed, take a stroll around the room and just take in what people have written or drawn on sticky notes.

5. Use your slide deck to show the images that you selected and invite reactions for each by using the following prompts.

Windows and Mirrors Follow-Up

- What kinds of windows were not represented in the lists that were generated? Think about different professions or events (police line-up) that utilize a more specialized type of window. Consider windows that are built to prevent crime or strong winds.
- What kinds of mirrors were not represented in the lists that were generated? Consider the fun house mirrors that you might encounter in a circus or amusement park. What about miniature mirrors that are specifically used in makeup kits? Consider mirrors that are adorned with lights.
- Does window size determine how much you can see if you are on the inside looking out?
- Brainstorm additional questions using the windows and mirrors metaphor.

ACTIVITY 2: WINDOWS AND MIRRORS – WHAT DO I SEE?

Staging: Prepare a space and seating arrangement that maximizes interaction. Use the slide deck from Activity 1.

Goals: Mastering the Windows and Mirrors framework for cross-cultural awareness and understanding. Build a helpful framework through which one can articulate experiences of other cultures.

Suggested steps:
    1. Prompts for Window Slideshow

- Imagine you are on the outside looking through the selected window in the slide.
- Describe what you might see and what, if anything, limits your vision.
- Compare this window to other windows in the presentation.
- Choose the window that you liked the best and explain why

    2. Prompts for Mirror Slideshow

- Imagine you are looking at your own reflection through the different kinds of mirrors you see.
- Describe the ways in which each mirror distorts or enhances what is reflected.
- Choose the mirror you preferred and explain why.

Windows and Mirrors Follow-Up

- Facilitate a discussion on how this exercise could help you to look at your life in different ways. How does it connect to how we view others or different issues?
- Discuss and describe the windows and mirrors you use to see the world and yourself in everyday life.

CHAPTER 2
CULTURE'S CALLING

Wander away into the unknown depths of this world and let your soul be your guide.

RUMI

When people ask me what I do, I proudly respond that I am a teacher and an educational leader whose passion is helping students of any age connect their life to some action that makes them better people. If indeed, as Gandhi stated, that change starts with us, then helping people must be my starting point. Usually, this proclamation is met with one of two responses, "Wow…how do you deal with kids all day long?" or "Teachers don't get paid what they deserve!" Neither response even remotely captures the deep love I have for a profession that has taken me around the globe and back again. Educators are among the most compassionate and altruistic people in our society. The work demands resilience, inextinguishable optimism, patience, and a belief that there are always ways to inspire any learner. An effective teacher is part pioneer. The crafting of diurnal command performances for audiences of myriad personalities forces us to develop and refine our ability to innovate. Most of us enter the profession exuberantly, believing that our lessons, words, and actions can inspire students to lead self-actualized (Maslow, 1943) lives and to serve our world for the better. I have wonderful teacher friends across the generations and disciplines. Those who remain dedicated seem to share an inextinguishable spark that burns like a flame in their eyes when they talk about their profession.

In an era where standardized testing often drives curricular choices, teachers must be people of vision and courage. Teaching suffers when doing what is best for kids exits the conversation and renders pedagogy a scripted endeavor. Global awareness and inter-cultural skills are priorities in our 21st century world. My passion for designing transformational learning (Mezirow, 1978) experi-ences is anchored in the hope that my students reach a deeper understanding of themselves while learning to see the world through the eyes of the "other." In doing so, they may glean a new insight, add a tool to their life skill toolbox, or allow their world-view to be altered in some subtle or profound way. There are few aspects of teaching more rewarding than the reciprocity between teacher and student.

The activities and insights in this book are not relegated to a specific population, age, or discipline. I have used them in corpo-rate training, youth leadership and advisory programs, travel orientations, creative writing, language courses, and DEIB initia-tives. The experiences within these pages are worth grappling with and aim only to move us all in the direction of stewarding a better world. They are, at once, both globally focused and highly person-alized. Of the many universal messages are timeless lessons that include:

- Building an appreciation for the deep structure, syntax, and semantics of language.

- Understanding how purposeful and mindful travel opens portals to new worlds and perspectives.
- Adopting a shared responsibility to care for our world through global partnerships and friendships.
- Celebrating and openly sharing both our differences and similarities.
- Applying principles and learnings to inspire innovative thinking and action in solving the challenges outlined in the United Nations Sustainable Development Goals (SDG).
- Filling the chasms of misunderstanding that often exist between cultural groups.

Early in my career as a teacher, I worked alongside well-meaning educators who wore their "language purist" approaches to instruction as a badge. Their insistence centered on the notion that learning the syntax of a language trumped all and was far more important than understanding the culture of those that speak it. I trumpet the converse. I speak three languages, and while learning the phrases, conjugations, and grammar points are essential, doing so without gaining a rich insight into culture is akin to baking a succulent pie to feast solely on the crust. As a profession, we are still learning the skill sets and nuances that are integral to teaching our students to be global stewards and citizens. Sadly, in some circles, the honorable idea of a global citizenry is often criticized by political ideologues and used as a talking point to inflame a misguided notion that cultural understanding somehow detracts from love for one's own country. These are often the same camps that don't see a value in learning languages and view English as the sacrosanct tongue that all inhabitants of the planet should speak. To take such an insular view is damaging; it shelters our children from profoundly life-changing experiences. Cultural superiority and xenophobia aren't specific to any one country and all of us can grow immensely by learning about others.

TEXTBOOK AND DIGITAL CULTURE

As a high school and undergraduate student, I "learned" French and Spanish using textbooks and basic Audio Lingual Method (ALM) methodology. These traditional practices served as a foundation for offering students a coherent, logical, and insipid introduction to language. It wasn't until my graduate years at World Learning's SIT Graduate Institute that my eyes and ears were awash with dynamic revolutionary pedagogical approaches to teaching language and culture: *The Silent Way, Total Physical Response, The Natural Approach, and Community Language Learning.* Earl Stevick's, *A Way and Ways,* remains a classic primer on these multiple approaches.

Yet, some decades post my graduate study, there are still far too many textbooks or tech-based classes in mainstream language learning. The rote memorization of phrases still exists as the arthritic backbone of pedagogy. As I shift my focus from language learning to teaching culture, this backbone shows even more telltale signs of disfigurement and degeneration. The cultural information presented in the typical middle or high school textbook is characterized by three root limitations:

1. Culture is often downsized to a small narrative note on the bottom of a page. It typically manifests as a brief, bland narrative called a "culture note" in which a concept such as the "importance of family" or "the bullfight" is described in highly simplistic terms.
2. Cultural vignettes are often presented in a random, disconnected manner giving one the feeling that learning about culture is of minor or secondary importance.
3. Real-world cultural diversity is so rich, layered, and varied that any attempt to "capture" or "cover" it in a curriculum will always fall short. The important recognition is that learners understand that an author (including me) has a

limited viewpoint based on one's own upbringing, circumstances, and cultural history. Knowing that we are all ignorant is a launchpad to lifelong learning and cultivation of a growth mindset (Dweck, 2006).

At best, a textbook serves as a unifying structure, and one way to position curricular scope and sequence. The best learning often takes place beyond the confines of those pristinely bound pages. Teachers and students are the collaborators that breathe life and meaning into activities. Student engagement animates our lessons and inspires teachers to find new ways to challenge them.

I am a pragmatic idealist. The genesis in my lesson plan design is the question, "How would I teach this topic in an ideal world?" I approach the planning of a lesson as if my four classroom walls were not barriers from the world outside and as if the perennial financial obstacles of budgets did not exist. In writing this book, I was motivated by several essential questions:

1. In most of the language, literature, and history classrooms, whose language and culture do we teach? Are we aware of the biases we have toward any country or region?
2. What are the "ideal" methodologies that allow K-adult learners to "experience" a culture given the physical constraints and confines of a classroom?
3. What is my working definition of culture? How can I ensure that cultural traits, norms, artistic expressions, mores, and worldviews supersede the teaching of statistics, folklore, flag colors, etc.?
4. How can I utilize my teacher role to dispel stereotypes and help students become more aware of their own culture and the cultural realities that have influenced their cognitive and cultural development?

What exactly is culture's call for help? The Washington Post reported U.S. Census data from 2019 that only 20% of Americans can converse in two or more languages and that compared with 56% of Europeans." This combined with estimates of only 30% of the U.S. population holding passports gives credence to the notion that we are limited in our ability to be fully immersed in other countries and cultures. This is not a critique, but a reality and often there are opportunity and fiscal factors that contribute to these numbers. To extrapolate, a vast majority of our students have never stepped beyond the safe confines of their hometown. They rely on us to design lessons that serve as "opportunities" to see world cultures through fresh eyes unencumbered by the blurred vision of stereotypes. Although stereotypes simplify the world around us, they are too often based on falsehoods. This book, at its best, is an attempt to provide "tabula rasa" experiences that develop our cultural meta-cognition. Epiphanies in the learning process are welcome events. Every lesson we design should be artfully rendered and skillfully enacted. Often, we treat the teachable moment as a rare event, when in essence it is **always** there for us to seize upon or ignore.

There are many dedicated and mission-driven organizations that devote their time and resources to promoting cultural under-standing. I have curated an exhaustive list of the most exemplary ones at teachlearnlead.net. The United Nations took a major step in bringing the global community together to galvanize around the 17 Sustainable Development Goals. On their website, they boldly state: "The Sustainable Development Goals are a universal call to action to end poverty, protect the planet and improve the lives and prospects of everyone, everywhere. The 17 Goals were adopted by all UN Member States in 2015, as part of the 2030 Agenda for Sustainable Development which set out a 15-year plan to achieve the Goals. Today, progress is being made in many places, but, over-all, action to meet the Goals is not yet advancing at the speed or scale required. 2020 needs to usher in a decade of ambitious action to deliver the Goals by 2030." The goals include:

1. No Poverty
2. Zero Hunger
3. Good Health and Well Being
4. Quality Education
5. Gender Equality
6. Clean Water and Sanitation
7. Affordable and Clean Energy
8. Decent Work and Economic Growth
9. Industry, Innovation, and Infrastructure
10. Reduced Inequalities
11. Sustainable Cities and Communities
12. Responsible Consumption and Production
13. Climate Action
14. Life Below Water
15. Life on Land
16. Peace, Justice, and Strong Institutions
17. Partnerships for the Goals

CHAPTER 3
STEROTYPES AND CULTURAL IDENTITY

"Learn to make yourself akin to people…. But let this sympathy be not with the mind – for it is easy with the mind – but with the heart, with love towards them."

VIRGINIA WOOLF

n a politicized and polarized world, it is difficult to find a cross-section of people that agree on their interpretations of specific issues. In fact, I often start a cultural lesson by asking my students to enumerate five things or concepts that represent the culture of the United States. Their answers, often, are quite different as they are operating with very specific experiences of a culture they know. If I ask the same set of students to describe their perceptions of people from other countries, the disparity becomes crystal clear. Their answers, unlike in the first question about the United States, are much closer to being the same and rarely based on empirical evidence. The similarity in responses is based on an overall lack of hard data or first-hand experience thus their impressions are more generalized. The roots of their "knowledge" are based on opinion and the phenomenon of stereotypes.

Harvard researchers (Bordalo et al., 2015) posited, "Stereotypes highlight differences between groups, and are especially inaccurate (consisting of unlikely, extreme types) when groups are similar. Stereotypical thinking implies overreaction to information that generates or confirms a stereotype, and underreaction to information that contradicts it. Stereotypes can change if new information changes the group's most distinctive trait." The notion of stereotyping and the role of media in cultivating stereotypes has long been both a personal and professional interest of mine. On a personal level, my family lines extend from Bahia Blanca, Argentina to Ascoli Piceno, Italy. My love for languages – especially Spanish and Italian – is a direct result of cultural immersion and of course food! I attended elementary and secondary school in a part of the southern United States that did not have a diverse representation of cultures. Although the prejudice I faced was often couched in humor and microaggressions, it was reflective of misconceptions people had of me as being part of an out-group in a corner of the country where the in-group was white, southern males.

I am proud to live in a multi-cultural and multi-generational household. My wife, an only child from Vietnam, my daughter, and I lived communally with my father-in-law until his passing at 103 years old. His forced relocation during the war from his Vietnamese homeland happened so late in his life that he was never able to learn English or carve out a career for himself here in the states. I have witnessed the painful struggles of my wife over the years. She came to the United States after bouncing from Guam to Arkansas to Florida as a refugee from the Vietnam War. She recounts stories of her American elementary school teachers butchering her Vietnamese name so badly that she was forced to adopt the name "Suzie" just to fit in and be recognized. Conversely, my daughter grew up in boarding schools from kindergarten through college and had roommates and friends from every corner of the world.

These experiences had a significant impact on her and how she sees this world for the amazing tapestry of cultures that it is. At this point in her life as a well-traveled 20-year-old, my daughter is better equipped for the modern world of work than any other generation of our family was.

In 2019, I was invited to be a delegate to Cote D'Ivoire, and this would be my first trip to the African continent. I was excited to enter a part of the world that I knew so little about. I failed to do my due diligence of research and learned that Cote D'Ivoire is a fully Francophone culture and I wasn't prepared to have language barriers during the trip. I also noted that a family member of the government official that hosted me was present at my side wher-ever I roamed. I was used to this and later learned that it was not only a cultural gesture, but also out of concern for my safety. I learned from local Ivorians that many people had formulated stereotypes about me as an outsider.

As a career teacher and school leader, I have found strength and great lessons in my own experiences growing up and in my many treks living abroad and trying to experience the world from the inside/out learning. My use of the term inside/out learning is meant to draw a clear distinction from learning about other cultures from the outside/in. I have highlighted some of the differ-ences in these learning modalities in the chart that follows.

INSIDE/OUT LEARNING	OUTSIDE/IN LEARNING
Living in another country in a homestay context.	Studying about another country and culture only through classroom study.
Living abroad as a full-time employee for an international school or organization.	Reading about international work in a manual or as related to you from someone who did it previously.
Learning another language while in the native country.	Learning a language in a classroom/ traditional textbook context.
Basing your knowledge of the mores and norms of another culture by using one's own cultural values and direct experiences.	Basing your knowledge and opinions of others solely on what books, media, or people tell us.
Seeking knowledge through conversations with a native of a given country you have interest in learning about.	Seeking knowledge through popular commercial media and based on the opinions of others.

I am not suggesting that all outside/in experiences are inadequate. For many people, the outside/in is all they may ever be able to access. Yet, even so, one should always strive to balance the outside/in with as many inside/out opportunities and experiences as possible.

SOCIAL IDENTITY THEORY AND STEREOTYPES

In any approach to pedagogy, specific theoretical frameworks are helpful to a teacher or trainer especially in one's effort to develop meaningful curriculum, activities, and projects. Tajfel (1969) wrote one of the most respected studies on the cognitive dimensions of prejudice. Although his work was not specifically focused on media, it was influential on researchers and theorists that focused on media and the perpetuation of stereotypes. Tajfel is credited with being the father of Social Identity Theory. According to Tajfel, "people categorize themselves and others in different groups and they evaluate these groups with the aim to reach a positive social identity...they tend to overemphasize the advantages and the supe-riority of the in-group." There are several interesting lectures avail-able on the Internet that go deeper into Social Identity Theory. I recommend you search the key terms below to find out more. This is but one lens through which we can better understand the complex nature of stereotypes. Key Terms for Internet Searches:

- Tajfel and Social Identity Theory
- Social Identity Theory – Lectures
- Steele – Stereotype Threat
- Model Minority Studies

STEREOTYPES – FRAMING KEY CONCEPTS TO INSPIRE DISCOURSE

Another effective way to teach awareness about stereotypes and the effects of media programming is to frame pedagogy in terms of tangible key concepts regarding stereotypes. There are many such concepts for consideration. In my research, I have found that the following three (stereotype threat, stereotype lift, and downward social comparison) tend to be cited most often in educational and sociological literature. Steele (1997) coined the term "stereotype threat" which refers to an individual member of a group that worries about being perceived as conforming to a negative stereo-type attributed to his or her group. For example, as an Italian American, some people may see me as having incessant cravings for pasta or familial ties to some unsavory characters popularized in media. The idea that all Asians belong to a "model minority" might also be an example of this. Although the model minority status can be a positive attribute, it tends to penalize Asian children that don't fit that profile.

Walton and Cohen (2003) identified the term "stereotype lift" as the "boost in performance caused by comparing oneself to a negatively stereotyped group." This is a typical case of one social or ethnic group feeling superior to another. This orientation, sadly, is evident in many parts of our society. To illustrate, consider class distinctions between the very wealthy and the very poor. In addition, one could argue that political pundits, on both sides, engage in stereotype lift daily on their shows when they demonize ideologically different political groups. Finally, Willis (1981) spoke of "downward social comparison" as the way in which members of a group boost their self-esteem or collective view of themselves by comparing their lot to a less fortunate group. If a teacher wishes to make an impact on disarming negative stereotypes, it is essential to equip students with some of the lexicon of concepts (as well as many others). By doing this, students can begin to look at examples in the media through specific lenses.

TEACHER NIRVANA

I count among the best experiences of my career the ten summers I directed the Program for International Education (P.I.E.) at The Putney School. Our international residential program was divided into two-month long sessions of intensive language and cultural studies. The work was generative, challenging, and inspirational. Given the intensity and brevity of the program, our ability to establish trust with and connection to our students had to be immediate. Each session, I collaborated with my team to create a thematic experiential program from scratch. There were no parameters placed on our design or on the creative process. We were solely responsible for the quality of educational and cultural experiences of our diverse international students. We had the liberating luxury to rid our mental backpacks of textbook-prescribed scope and sequence, and our working lexicon was free from standardized test edu-speak. Craft and collaboration trumped all.

We scrapped what didn't work, assessed students on an ongoing basis, incessantly reflected upon the assumptions we made, and held steadfast to the experiential and progressive mission of the program. We lived and breathed P.I.E. because it epitomized shared values and an unabashed belief that cultural understanding inspires empathy and mutual respect. I never thought of my time at the helm of P.I.E. as work. We committed ourselves to planning around the clock by choice, and lessons were free from departmental or academic discipline constraints. Our goals were clear. We sought innovative ways to design experiential curriculum (including a school on wheels) that pushed our students to learn the English language, experience U.S. culture, and better understand themselves and each other. The diverse student body, ephemeral nature of their time with us and our pursuit of shared mission and vision made our *canicular days* collaborations profound and indescribably rewarding. My experiences at The Putney School inspired me to radically rethink and reconfigure what I did in the classroom.

RATIONALE AND ASSUMPTIONS

In the pursuit of cultural understanding, it is not sufficient to merely study the "other." Students should be provided opportunities to explore their own culture and will benefit immensely by learning how their cultural upbringing influences the way they perceive the world and process information about behaviors and practices that are culturally different from their own. In the world language classroom, we are often guilty of teaching culture in a vacuum even though we know that there are better, more effective ways of reaching our students. Culture is alive, vibrant, perplexing, and controversial yet often it is taught in ways that make it seem dead, predictable, and mind-numbingly simplistic. Before one embarks upon learning about other cultures, it is imperative to embrace the role of humility in the process. Detaching, even temporarily, from our ethnocentric beliefs is equal parts painful and liberating. Teaching cultural understanding is akin to holding a mirror up to the world and managing not to lose sight of one's reflection in every image we see.

Experiential learning weaves simulation, reflection, introspective inquiry, discussion, and real-world interaction to engage learners at the most personal level possible. As students learn more about themselves, the hope is that they gain the empathy, ethic of curiosity, and global literacy necessary to be skillful citizens ready for whatever the 21st century tosses in their path. In his classic, Democracy and Education, Dewey wrote extensively about a learners' most basic relationship with an educational experience:

> The first stage of any contact with any new material, at whatever age of maturity, must inevitably be of the trial-and-error sort. An individual must try, in play or work, to do something with material in carrying out his own impulsive activity, and then note the interaction of his energy and that of the material employed. This is what happens when a child first begins to build with blocks, and it is equally what happens when a scientific man in his laboratory begins to experiment with unfamiliar objects. Hence the first approach to any subject in school, if thought is to be aroused and words not acquired should be as un-scholastic as possible.

In the visuals below, I have included both Kurt Lewin's "Experiential Education" cycle and Dewey's "Experiential Continuum" Model.

Concrete
experience

Testing implications
of concepts in
new situations

Observations
and
reflections

Formation of
abstract concepts
and generalizations

PAST   PRESENT   FUTURE
DEWEY'S EXPERIENTIAL CONTINUUM

Every experience is shaped by each experience that came before it and leaves a
residue that influences every experience that comes in the future.
This is also referred to as continuity of experience.

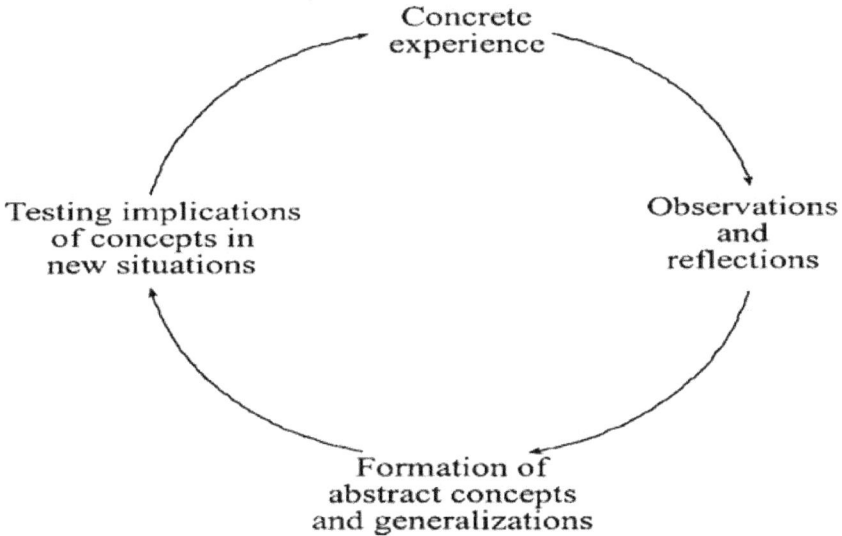

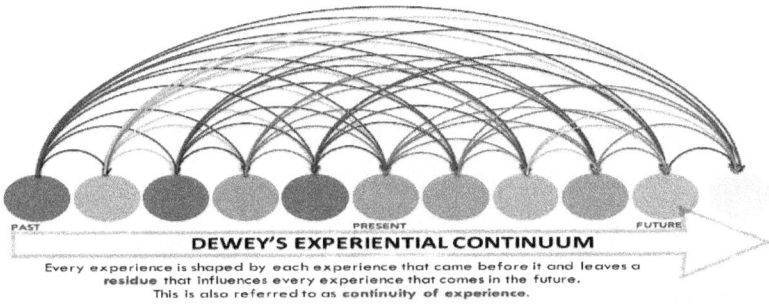

ACTIVITY 3: SOCIAL IDENTITY THEORY

Staging: Pen, pencil, paper, journals or computers, teacher background knowledge of Social Identity Theory (SIT). The deeply personal nature of this activity makes it potentially very powerful. The teacher must establish ground rules about the importance of respecting others' opinions and perspectives. The teacher serves as a facilitator throughout the discussions that emerge.

Goals: Add additional frameworks to your toolbox for cultural understanding.

Suggested Steps

1. After presenting the tenets of SIT, ask students to consider their own affiliation with social groups. Students should begin with individual reflection essays on any of the following prompts:
2. To which social group(s) do you most closely belong? Why do you belong to this group?
3. Identify an in-group at your current school or workplace. Explain who belongs to this group. Why do you consider it an in-group? Are you a member of this group? Could you ever be a member of this group?
4. Identify an out-group at your current school or workplace. Explain who belongs to this group. Why do you consider it an out-group? Are you a member of this group? Could you ever be a member of this group? Would you want to be a member?

Windows and Mirrors Follow-Up:

- Consider ways in which student writing and ensuing discussions can be sustained throughout your course.
- Could you utilize the data they provide to help design statements about classroom culture and climate?
- This a wonderful way to connect with your students and glean insight about (a) social groups in your schools and (b) their own individual experiences of being members of in/out groups.

ACTIVITY 4: CULTURE CLASH

Staging: Journals to record observations. Students will need places to record information and observations. This activity works best if you have a teaching partner as students will be divided into two groups.

Goals: Gaining insights on decoding unfamiliar cultural behaviors. Risk-taking as it relates to crossing culture. Developing strategies for dealing with cultural dissonance and confusion. Heightened awareness of one's own behaviors when entering another country and culture.

Suggested Steps:

1. Consider leading a brief discussion with students about any travels they have had to other countries. Try to get a sense of what their experiences were like and of the trip context, e.g., vacation, camp, service, visit relatives. Encourage storytelling and contribute some tales of your own.

2. Divide students into two equally (if possible) numbered groups. In a class of 20, for example, assign them to two groups of ten. Each group should go off with their teacher leader for the period. They should be warned not to speak to the other group about what they are doing until the activity is complete. After groups are separated, each teacher leader should explain that they will have a full class period to learn and internalize the rules and norms of a new culture. The teacher provides each group with a detailed description of the culture on an index card. *For two examples*, please refer to Culture 1 and Culture 2 descriptions on p. 28.

There are a host of questions that are integrated into this experience. You will see them on the following pages. Please note that you should allow your creative juices to flow with the Staging of this experience. Choose your physical spaces wisely and be sure to have plenty of support from team members or student leaders. Although the descriptions of each culture have been created specifically for this activity, you should take liberty to alter or modify any of the behaviors, attitudes, and norms that typified each manufactured group.

CULTURE 1 (Group 1)
In your culture, all is communicated through gestures and pictures. You are a people who are very proud of its art and artistic talents. It seems, however, that only people with brown or black hair are permitted to draw. The others are only permitted to use gestures. You are often frightened by people with loud voices, and you try to avoid them at all costs. When you draw or use gestures, it is considered polite for the person listening to giggle softly, nod his/her head or tap you lightly on the arm. You are a friendly people.

CULTURE 2 (Group 2)
In your culture, all is communicated through voice. You have different tones that express different feelings. When you whisper, you are very confused. When you speak loudly you are generally very happy. When you hum or sing you are often very upset or frustrated. There is no written language in your culture. You are not a visual people but rather a very physical people. You find laughter to be very offensive unless there is direct eye contact.

3. Both groups should work quietly (and always separately) in opposite ends of a campus or building. It is imperative that each group keep their culture a secret during this time. Students collaborate by reading their index cards carefully and working together to decipher the habits and behaviors of their new culture. They practice and rehearse the behavioral norms. Before the next class meeting, each teacher leader must inform their respective groups that they will meet in separate locations again for one more class session.

4. On day 2, each teacher leader should give their groups one final chance to rehearse their behaviors and assume their respective roles and personas. Next, divide your group of ten into five distinct pairs. These pairs will leave the room in 5-minute increments to visit the other culture. Simultaneously, pairs from the other group will visit your room. Finally, read the following instructions:

5. When told to begin, send participants in pairs to visit another culture. The task is to welcome visitors in another culture. Use powers of observation and intuition to learn as much as they can in your 5-minute visit. The culture you visit may be very different, and it may not be easy (or even possible) to communicate. Do not get frustrated, but rather do your best to learn as much as you can about the other people in the room. Be careful about the conclusions you draw. When you return to your home culture, you will have 1 - 2 minutes to debrief us on what you have learned. After your two minutes have elapsed, we will send off the next pair.

6. Develop a plan for participants who might detract or fully give their best during this experience. The activity is easily undermined by anyone that does not take it seriously whether it be divulging confidential "cultural" secrets to the other team of visitors or simply not being willing to stay in character. I suggest having an honest and open conversation before the activity begins and perhaps for the rare participant who does not want to "play a role" you could offer them the chance to be an objective observer and note-taker.

7. After every pair has had the chance to visit and debrief, bring all students back together. The fun begins at this point. Allow students from Culture 1 to make some guesses as to why Culture 2 behaves as it does. It is up to Culture 2 to confirm, validate or deny these conjectures. The same should be done with Culture 2. Give these students a chance to comment on Culture 1. When this has been completed, the final session can take place.

Windows and Mirrors Follow-Up
In this session, students are asked to think of this experience in broader terms. For example, I have found the following questions to be quite helpful:

- How many of you have traveled to countries or places where the language and culture were different than your own?
- What are some of the things you did to understand that culture and the behaviors you observed?
- Would any of you like to share a story related to this topic?
- Do you think that people who visit or immigrate to the United States ever experience this kind of confusion?
- What would you say is the most perplexing/confusing thing about U.S. culture? How would you help a visitor, or a new immigrant make sense of this confusion?
- Consider journaling on this experience today. What emotions or feelings do you recall experiencing? What lessons or insights did you learn as you participated as both cultural expert and visitor.
- If you were to travel to another country, what things would you do to prepare for such an experience?
- What tricks and strategies did you use or invent to be able to communicate?

ACTIVITY 5: ALL FROGS CROAK

Staging: Easel with poster size paper or a large smart board/white board. Markers. Pen, paper, journals or approved devices for participants to record personal reflections, information, and observations.
Goals: Awareness of the ways in which humans assign stereotypes to different groups and artifacts. Cultural understanding of the

conveyance of stereotypes through media channels. Self-knowledge as to the judgments you make about people and things on a regular basis.

Suggested Steps

This is a robust and poignant activity when done carefully. Your facilitation skills are perhaps most essential as discussions can become spirited and unfocused without strong teacher guidance.

1. You might consider enacting some ground rules about sharing and respecting viewpoints of others. This activity can often be provocative, but it is essential not to censor what people believe. In addition, this activity makes participants aware of how our cultural upbringing has the power to shape and influence our perceptions of the world.

2. Use the groups I have listed or make a similar list of your own. Display the names of the groups using your choice of media (projector, white board, post-its). Instruct your students to silently look at the names of the groups. Depending on the ages of participants, you might alter the mix of subjects. Here is a sample list:

- Immigrants
- Politicians (Republicans, Democrats, Independents, Green Party)
- Professions (Sanitation Workers, Librarians, Teachers, IT, Farmers, Jazz Musicians)
- Tribes (Metal Heads, Yuppies, Rednecks, Hipsters)
- The Homeless and Unhoused population
- Geographical Markers (Northerners, Southerners, Midwesterners, Europeans)

3. Ask students to privately list what comes to mind when they think of these groups. If students have never heard of one of the groups, it is appropriate for them to leave a blank space.

4. If possible, list each group header at a different spot in your

classroom. Invite students (*you may want to have them all stand at once to lower the inhibition level*) to visit each group area and instruct them to write some of their descriptions under each group heading. This task normally takes ten minutes.

5. When everyone has returned to their seat, lead a discussion about the descriptions and why students chose the words they did. Ask students to share whether their descriptions were based on any of the following criteria:

- Based on first-hand experience.
- Based on what people have told me.
- Based on media depiction.
- Based on someone who has self-identified as one or more these groups have stated about themselves.

Windows and Mirrors Follow-Up:
Assign some significant time for reflective writing. Ask participants to imagine that they are walking through a large park in a country where absolutely no one looks or sounds like them. As you interact with different people, write separate journal entries/essays from the point of view of the three different people that you met and who seem to be staring at you. Here is a sample list of people from whose perspectives you should write:

- An elderly man on a park bench who you asked for directions.
- A young child on a scooter chasing pigeons in the plaza.
- A pop-up vendor who sold you some fresh fruit and bottled water.
- A beggar who approached you seeking money.
- Two businesswomen whose conversation you interrupted by sitting near them on a bench.

ACTIVITY 6: SO...HOW MANY LANGUAGES DO YOU SPEAK?

Staging: Either a digital display or an easel with poster size paper. Markers. Pen, paper, journals, or approved devices for participants to record personal reflections, information, and observations.

Goals: Strengthening research skills on the topic of languages. Understanding one's language proficiency as it relates to the mosaic of languages spoken worldwide. Awareness of the threat of language extinction and how it relates to cultures vanishing.

Suggested Steps:

1. Ask participants how many languages are spoken in their families. Create a list that represents the collective. Solicit estimates of how many documented languages there are in the world and introduce concepts such as official language, dialects, ethnocentricity, xenophobia, polyglots, bilingualism.

2. Unveil a visual that represents the names of every language in the world that has between 500,000 and 1 million speakers. Consult sites such as Ethnologue for accurate information on human languages and language rankings.

3. Take time to read the expansive list and ask participants to stop you when they recognize a familiar language name. Prod participants to share how they know the language or the connection they have to it.

4. Typically, there are anywhere from 15-20 languages that are familiar to an audience, but the vast number are ones that participants have never heard of until this activity. Encourage students to capture an image with their phone cameras of the expansive list in the hope that It becomes a symbolic reminder as to why we study language and how much more there is out there to learn.

5. We have only mentioned languages that have between 500,000 and 1 million speakers. Did you know that experts estimate that there are between 2500 and 7500 languages in the world?

- Are you surprised by the number of languages there are in the world?
- How does this information make you feel? Are you overwhelmed? Are you underwhelmed?
- Do you want to learn more languages? Are you happy that your language is one that is widely used?
- Every year languages (like animals) face extinction. Does this surprise you? Alarm you?
- What do you think would cause a language to become extinct?
- How does each language you learn impact how much you know about a given culture or community that speaks it?

Windows and Mirrors Follow-Up:

- Select three languages from the list that intrigue you, and research these languages (using the Internet, library, and / or interviews with native speakers) with respect to where they are spoken, who speaks to them. What are the various words to express "hello," "peace," "learn," "community" and "friendship?"
- What are the languages currently in danger of extinction? Is it inevitable or are actions being taken to preserve such languages?
- In the context of windows and mirrors, what are connections you can make to the study and learning of a new language with the windows we use to see the world and other cultures?
- Describe the ways in which our native language is both a window and mirror?
- Research the study of linguistics by learning about terms such as semantics, syntax, phonemes, etc. and distribute visuals of how and where sounds are made in the mouth.

Consider using the book <u>The Language Files</u> (Bergman, Hall, Ross 2007) as your resource.

- What are the ways AI, ChatGBT, and other technological innovations influence the learning of languages?

ACTIVITY 7: LIVING ON AZTEC AND MAYAN TIME

Staging: Aztec and Mayan Calendars – variety of blank copies available on the Internet. Pen, paper, journals or approved devices for participants to record personal reflections, information, and observations.

Goals: Developing cultural understanding and heightened awareness of how different cultures mark time.

Schema Activation: Consider leading a discussion on time. How do we mark its passing? Why do we measure days, months, years, minutes, and hours as we do? Try to inspire some critical thought and reasoning skills on this topic.

Suggested Steps:

1. Introduce this activity when you present any of the following concepts: seasons, dependence on weather, physical geography, literature with protagonists that live in an agrarian or developing nation. Building on your schema activation discussions, challenge students to answer the following questions:

- What instruments or tools do we use to tell time?
- What do we use to keep track of important dates?
- Do you think that all cultures organize time as we do in the United States?

2. Invariably, in answering the first question above, a student

will say, "We use our phones, watches, and calendars to tell time and organize time." At this point, call on volunteers to draw a typical calendar on the board. Usually, they draw a very linearly organized calendar.

3. Present students with a picture of an Aztec or Mayan Calendar. Ask them to make some guesses as to what it is and what it might represent. Students may be remotely familiar with the structure depending on previous learning.

4. Encourage students to make conjectures about how the circular calendar was used. Research the calendars yourself prior to the activity and use your lecture notes to fill in any gaps in your students' collective knowledge. Provide blank templates of an aztec or Mayan calendar. Provide the following directions:

> You now have your own blank copy of an Aztec or Mayan calendar. You have the remaining time in class to draw symbols inside the calendar that represent you and the way you organize and spend your time. The center circle should depict something that represents you or the culture in which you were raised. The remaining parts of the calendar can be designed as you wish. I am not judging you on your artistic talents but strive to be neat when you draw so that I can clearly see what you have created. In filling in all the parts of this calendar, try to think of why you are designing it as you have. I will ask you to explain it to me and perhaps, if you are comfortable doing so, to the entire class.

Some students will be very simple and concrete in the things they draw. This has no bearing on how I grade students. In doing this activity, I am mainly interested in two things: 1) that students recognize that the ways in which cultures measure time and events can be radically different, and 2) that students give me a glimpse into their lives and the things that they value most.

Collect all the calendars and "white-out" artist names. Redistribute the papers and present the students with the following scenario: Imagine that you are all anthropologists and archeologists. You have discovered the remains of a great civilization. Your job is to analyze the data that you have in front of you and to write a small paper as to what these calendars represent. Allow the students 20 minutes to guess the meanings of the symbols and to write a descriptive letter to the calendar's creator. The calendars are returned along with the letters to their owners.

Windows and Mirrors Follow-Up

- What do you use to mark time? A standard block calendar? A digital platform?
- After understanding the complexity of the Aztec calendar, what information does it capture that you do not presently have represented in your own calendar?
- If someone were to create an Aztec model for modern day life, what would a potential design be and what would be included and conveyed?

ACTIVITY 8: ONE PERSON, MANY NAMES

Staging: Device for research and recording data. Pen, paper, journals or approved devices for participants to record personal reflections, information, and observations.

Goals: A deeper awareness about the history and origins of names. Understanding the ways in which names can define us, especially in cultures where names have a very specific meaning attached to them.

Suggested Steps:
Craft a discussion around common names in our culture. Ask

students how much they know about their own names. Ask them to share their favorite names, i.e. "If your parents hadn't named you Biff, what name would you have chosen?" Encourage students to converse with their parents and grandparents about their names and why they chose as they did. Using the schema activation discussions as the impetus, assign the following questions for research:

- What is your full name? Does it have any specific meaning?
- What is the history of why this name was given to you?
- Does your middle name or surname have any specific meaning?
- Do you have a nickname? How did you get this nickname?
- If you could have named yourself, what would you be called? Why?

Windows and Mirrors Follow-Up

Facilitate a discussion in which participants can share their research with the group.

- Did you already know the meaning and history behind your name(s)?
- Does knowing the story behind your name(s) change the way you see yourself?
- Does learning about the names of other participants change the way you see or experience them?

ACTIVITY 9: 5 QUALITIES OF TEENS?

Staging: Journals or paper and pen. Slide show with images of contemporary teens, teen fashion, etc.

Goals: An open discussion about the ways in which teenagers are stereotyped in a culture. Increased awareness about the power of stereotypes to overgeneralize and stigmatize.

Suggested Steps:

Present the following scenario to your students: You have won a major student grant from the National Endowment for the Humanities to study in Uruguay. You will be the first NEH Fellow to live in and study in this region of Uruguay. As such, your grant requires that you prepare a major presentation on the topic of U.S. teen culture. You have been told that the presentation must be titled: "Five Qualities of a Typical Teenager in the United States."

- The presentation can take multiple formats and use any platforms that best serve to convey the information. Keep the instructions simple and open-ended. The topic is the topic!
- Explain to participants that they must bring five props, artifacts, or pieces of media research that represent and substantiate each of the five qualities. Set clear guidelines on presentation length.
- As participants submit their five qualities to the teacher, create a single collaborative document that everyone can access and comment on. Give participants a time frame by which any constructive comments are due.

Windows and Mirrors Follow-Up

- Did you note any patterns or themes emerging in the overall list of qualities or in the five you presented?
- Were your five qualities based on your personal preferences or are they more reflective of images/beliefs you think people have about teens?
- Was it difficult or easy to limit yourself to five qualities?

- Of the many presentations and qualities generated, did you have a strong reaction to any specific ones?

ACTIVITY 10: LANGUAGE IMMERSION EXPERIENCE

Staging: Journals or paper and pen. Reserve and stage a venue that has multiple rooms. Ideally a classroom, but this could be done outdoors if you have no other options. The key design feature is making separate stations for each language encounter.

Goals: Empathy for second and third language learners. Insights about how you react in situations that can be confusing and immersive. Potential interest in further learning one of the languages you were exposed to in the activity rotation.

Suggested Steps:

1. Prepare participants for a class or training session in which they will not hear or use their native language. To make this an effective activity, logistical preparation is essential. Assuming that we are working with a class period of 45 – 60 minutes, customize as necessary.

2. Contact teachers in your school or members of the community that fluently speak a language other than English. Invite them to give about 60 minutes of their time to a unique learning experience. Schedule six "teachers" for 5–8-minute increments and assign them to different places/rooms on your campus or in your building. Accompany your students to each location and remind them that their job is to learn and decode as much of the languages they experience as they can.

- **Block 1** – Visit Spanish classroom. Break to jot thoughts and reflections

- **Block 2** – Visit Vietnamese classroom. Break to jot thoughts and reflections
- **Block 3** – Visit Chinese classroom. Break to jot thoughts and reflections
- **Block 4** – Visit Turkish classroom. Break to jot thoughts and reflections
- **Block 5** – Visit Arabic classroom. Break to jot thoughts and reflections
- · **Block 6** – Visit Swahili classroom. Break to jot thoughts and reflections

Although fun, these types of immersive experiences can be exhausting and frustrating. Give participants ample time to decompress and make additional reflections.

Windows and Mirrors Follow-Up

Note: There are so many directions the post-experience can take. The following prompts are ones that I have personally experienced or facilitated.

- Give participants time to first discuss their collective experiences with each other and without any facilitator to guide their conversations.
- As you rejoin the group and begin facilitation, consider the following questions to promote more meaningful conversation.
- How did it feel to go from class to class and language to language?
- Did you persevere or shut down in any of the lessons?
- Were you motivated to understand the language, or did you feel frustrated?
- Were some languages easier to understand than others?
- What words or gestures do you recall learning?

- When you use English with a non-native speaker, do you think that he or she feels the same way you did?
- Is immersion an effective way to learn a language?
- Visit ethnologue.com get an accurate sense of the variety of languages spoken throughout the world.
- What are the determining factors that cultivate a country's need to have bilingual or multilingual citizens?

ACTIVITY 11: RELIGION AND THE CULTURAL ANTHROPOLOGIST

Staging: Pre-load the activity by sharing the Tulane site. Survey students to see if they are comfortable talking about their own religious upbringings as opposed to their beliefs. Consider a poster or some digital display in which you have a listing of 75 - 100 names of world languages.

Goals: Increased global awareness of religious practice and expression. Building self-confidence around articulating your own religious upbringing. (**Note**: there is a marked difference between objectively sharing a religious upbringing and a religious belief).

Suggested Steps

Explain to participants that religion and religious belief can be studied objectively without controversy or risk of offending others. Suggest taking on the role of a non-obtrusive journalist solely reporting what they see. Explore the career of cultural anthropology.

- Visit Tulane University's https://libguides.tulane.edu/religiousstudies/websites
- Study the Tulane webpage. Make note of the variety of religions and faith communities present.

- What are your immediate reactions? Are you surprised by the diversity of religious beliefs?
- When you are ready, identify a religion or faith community that you wish to research and that has no connection to your cultural, ethnic, or family history.
- Read the description about this religion and investigate the qualities or facets that have the most appeal to you as a seeker.
- Although they will need to note quantitative data such as numbers of followers and geographical locations where the religion is most prevalent, this is only surface information.
- Create a shared, collaborative document so that participants can have a section of the spreadsheet to add the name of the religion and some of the data they learned.
- Provide a forum for participants to speak to each other about what they researched and learned and why they chose the religion they did for this exercise.
- Facilitate a larger discussion that explores themes beyond the numbers. Suggestions appear below in the Windows and Mirrors discussion.

Windows and Mirrors Follow-Up

- What is the role, if any, that religion or religious belief has played in your life?
- Why do you think that you haven't heard of the religion you studied before this experience?
- Are you surprised at the number of religions that exist in the world today? Do you think there are more in the present day than in history?
- Of the religion you studied, who is attributed with founding it and what are its main tenets?

- Imagine that you are an adherent of this religion. How would you help explain your way of life and beliefs to someone that is curious about it and you?

ACTIVITY 12: MUSIC MIX

Staging: Device to play music samples.

Goals: Global awareness, Understanding culture through musical expression. Increasing one's knowledge of music genres and sub-genres.

Suggested Steps:

1. Discuss the fact that many people are comfortable listening to the music they like and do not necessarily show curiosity for new sounds. Explore how mainstream radio plays certain formats of music and doesn't stray from its formula. Introduce concepts like community radio, short-wave radio, college radio, and public radio to expose students to broader concepts of broadcasting in our culture and other cultures. If possible, provide examples using Internet streaming on your classroom computer, mobile device, or computer lab.

2. Ask students to make a list of all musical genres that they know or have heard of. Typically, this will result in a very limited list of 5 – 10 genres. At this point challenge students further by asking them to list sub-genres of music within the genres they named. Again, this tends to be very difficult for students that haven't previously thought about music in this way before.

3. The Musical Ear Test: Choose five audio samples from five different genres of music and play them while looking at the check-list below. Ask them to identify in order (1 - 5) musical genres they think they hear. Here is a sampling:

- Jazz
- Bluegrass
- Rap
- Dub
- Merengue

4. Once students have completed the task #1 and the Musical Ear Test, pair them up and guide them to create a collaborative document (Google Docs, Wiki, etc.). They should title this document "Music Mix" followed by their initials. Provide them with class time to collaborate in pairs and try to add to the lists they made individually.

5. Discuss the concepts of genres and sub-genres. Tell students that you are going to share an incomplete (but overwhelming) list of sub-genres comprising the "Pop/Rock" category.

Pop/Rock Genre and accompanying pop/rock sub-genres:

- College Rock
- Post-Disco
- Funk Metal
- Goth Metal
- Industrial Metal
- Punk Metal
- Rap-Metal
- Alternative Dance
- Ambient Pop
- Britpop
- Chamber Pop
- Cowpunk
- Emo
- Garage Punk
- Grunge
- Indie

- Lo-Fi
- Neo-Glam,
- Neo-Psychedelia
- Psychobilly
- Shoegaze
- Ska-Punk
- Space Rock
- Screamo
- Bubblegum, British Blues, Freakbeat, Merseybeat, Mod, Anarchist Punk,
- Oi!
- House
- Ragga
- Rave
- K-Pop
- Glitter
- Acid Rock
- Arena Rock
- Southern Rock
- Progressive Metal
- Jam Bands

***Note**: This is only one genre, and the list of subgenres is much longer.

In most cases, there is shock when participants see the length of the list. Try to glean whether they have heard of some of "Pop/Rock" subgenres on the previous list. Imagine the collective size of the lists if this same exercise were done with other genres of music.Introduce students to the allmusic.com platform and allow them to explore the genres and subgenres of music that exist in our culture and other cultures.

Windows and Mirrors Follow-Up

- Students could choose a few samples of a subgenre of music they have never heard before and share it with the group.
- What struck you about this music sample?
- What is your reaction in learning that there are thousands of forms and subgenres of musical expression?
- Provide an audio or video sample of something you listened to in an unfamiliar language that you really enjoyed. What made the tune catch your attention even though you don't understand the lyrics?
- Listen to a piece of music in a foreign language without translating and then again with a translation. What, if anything, changes when you do this?

CHAPTER 4
CULTURAL EXPERIENCES AND SIMULATIONS

The man who never alters his opinion is like standing water, and breeds reptiles of the mind.

WILLIAM BLAKE

A pre-test is a great baseline measure of one's literacy in any subject. You can easily tailor it to meet your own needs based on what you choose to focus on in a given discipline. This culture pretest was developed to measure a student's general knowledge of Latino and Hispanic culture. It is meant to be administered before studying any cultural topic and can be adapted to a topic of your choice. It is merely a way to measure preconceived notions that we all possess, and the questions are intentionally global in scope.

In creating a pretest, I had several factors to consider. I wondered what the test would reveal about a given set of participants. If they did poorly on the test, would this deflate their confidence? I found the contrary to be true. Test-takers are surprised to learn the actual answers to most questions. These "surprises" often translate to an increased desire to learn more and fill the "gaps" of one's knowledge base.

In an actual classroom setting of mine many years ago, the pretest served as a baseline guide. Many of my students could only answer about 20% of the questions correctly at the beginning of the year. As the school year progressed, I refer to the pre-test often and slowly we fill in the missing data. By the end of the year, my students are ready to take the test again, but this time they can answer close to 100% of the questions. Their confidence and sense of accomplishment soar and their cultural knowledge becomes something very tangible and concrete. Again, this pre-test is meant to be a template and can be used to assess any topic. Your design depends entirely on the content of your curriculum, presentation, or training. The technique is what matters most in setting up this activity.

ACTIVITY 13: THE CULTURE PRE-TEST

As I devised this test, I considered the following:

1. What do I think my students know about a given cultural topic?

2. Will low scores on the pre-test and high scores on the post-test help to motivate students and give them a sense of accomplishment?

3. Is my course or training designed in such a way that participants will know the answer to every question by the end of the course? Can the pre-test/post-test stimulate and motivate students to learn more about culture when they leave my classroom?

4. What are the other types of topics that you could create a pre-test for to deliver in a course, presentation, orientation, or training session. Brainstorm at least 3 and jot them down.

1. Topic Idea #1
2. Topic Idea #2

3. Topic Idea #3

Sample of a Cultural Knowledge Pre-Test

Instructions: You have 10 - 15 minutes to read through and answer as many of the following questions as you can. I cannot assist you unless your question is about test instructions. You are not receiving a grade for this test. It is for your eyes only unless you choose to share with a peer or colleague. Relax, give it your best effort, and use the results as a launchpad to learn. You may leave answers blank. Good luck!

1. Approximately how many native speakers of Spanish are there in the world? _____
2. Rank the following languages in order by the total number of native speakers worldwide. Use the numbers provided for you below.

English, Spanish, Arabic, Hindi, French, Chinese, Russian, German, Japanese, Bengali

#1_____
#2_____
#3_____
#4_____
#5_____

3. Which of the following minority groups in the United States comprises the largest percentage of our population?
  a) Asian
  b) African American
  c) Hispanic
  d) Native American

4. Which of the following Spanish-speaking countries is a territory of the United States?

a) Dominican Republic

b) Spain

c) Haiti

d) Puerto Rico

e) Cuba

5. How many countries have declared Spanish as their official language?

a) 5

b) 10

c) 15

d) 20

e) 21

f) 113

6. List as many countries from question #5 as you can.

7. Name as many luminaries of Hispanic heritage in each of the following categories.

ACTORS:

ATHLETES:

AUTHORS:

POLITICAL LEADERS:

ARTISTS:

INVENTORS:

8. Arguably, the vernacular English language has been greatly influenced by the Spanish language. Provide as many examples as you can of words, terms, and concepts that illustrate this argument.

9. What cities in the United States have the largest concentration of Spanish-speakers?

10. What parts of the United States belonged to Mexico at one time?

END OF PRE-TEST

ACTIVITY 14: THE MARKET EXPERIENCE PART 1 - CARIBBEAN FRUIT

Staging: If budget and geography permits, purchase an array of tropical fruits with an emphasis on exotic and lesser-known varieties. Prepare a slide deck or video clips of small fruit stands in the Caribbean islands.

Goals: Increased awareness of popular fruits in other countries. Exploration of agriculture and sustainability issues that many countries face. Historical awareness of the role agriculture has played in a local economy.

Suggested Steps:

1. Ask students to describe the concept "tropical." Explore the ways in which students shop for foods in the United States, e.g., how frequently do they go to a grocery store? Ask them to describe the size of a typical grocery store in the United States. What fruits are typically available?

2. If possible, do some advance research on local Hispanic markets in your region. Ideally, arranging a field experience with your students to the "bodega" or "colmado" is preferable, but if this is impossible logistically, provide your students with a list of some stores in the general area. Using the advice of a local expert, purchase a variety of exotic fruits and fruit juices.

3. Tell your students that you have brought them some surprises. Slowly take each fruit from a grocery bag and ask students to guess what it is. Encourage students to smell and touch the fruit.

4. Have students sketch a picture and record the names of each fruit in their notes or journals. Prompt them to write a description of the fruit that focuses on color, texture of the skin and the flesh.

Example: Papaya

SKETCH: (Sketch an image of what you see)
TEXTURE: (Describe the feel of it)
COLOR: (What is the primary color? Are there several colors? If so, are the colors associated with different parts of the fruit?)
SMELL: (How would you describe the smell of the skin? What about the inside or flesh of the fruit?
TASTE: (How would you describe the taste? Is it like any other fruit you have eaten previously? Would you buy this fruit in the future is available?

5. Explain the concept of an open-air produce market. Draw comparisons to seasonal farmers' markets in the United States but be sure to make clear contrasts where appropriate. For example, the open-air food markets I visited in the Dominican Republic and Puerto Rico tend to be a daily shopping experience for people. They are often located in the center of small towns and villages, and are places where people congregate, socialize, and shop daily for fresh produce and meats. This is rarely the case of the typical farmers' markets in the United States as they tend to be seasonal, ephemeral (i.e., set up/taken down the same day), and not the sole source of food shopping. It is essential to help students recognize these distinctions.

6. Ask participants to share any stories about their own travels and experiences with markets like the ones highlighted in this activity.

Windows and Mirrors Follow-Up

- Do you know any local farmers or farmers markets?
- Have you ever been to an open-air market?

- How does your family do most of its shopping? Do you shop daily? Weekly?
- What are some of the pros and cons of shopping daily for food as people in many countries do?

ACTIVITY 15: THE MARKET EXPERIENCE PART 2 - CARIBBEAN LIFE

Staging: Slides on international ads for markets and stores, screenshots of banner ads for specialized stores, images of various open-air markets or small shops from any countries you choose.

Goals: Exploration of commerce, agriculture, and sustainability issues globally. Connect to United Nations SDG's. Provide a historical and cultural context for the role small businesses have played in local economies worldwide.

Suggested Steps:

Reflect upon the experience that students had in Market Experience Part 1. Revisit the ways in which students shop for foods in the United States, but now open the conversation to all kinds of shopping. Use examples of online stores, big box stores, malls, and specialty shops in urban centers and small-town downtown areas. What do these types of shopping have in common? How are they different? Explore the concepts of bartering and bargaining.

- Share photographs of open-air markets around the globe. If possible, see if anyone can identify countries or regions with each photo they view.
- Provide resources for students to research on how agriculture is a key part of the economic engine of countries.

- Challenge students to find examples of other kinds of small market stands in other countries. For example, in my many travels throughout Puerto Rico and the Dominican Republic, I found the following types of stands to be commonplace in both roadways and plaza style open-air markets:

1. Butcher shops
2. Fresh flower shops
3. Cafeteria-style family restaurants
4. Fresh fruit vendors
5. Fresh vegetable vendors
6. Fresh fruit shake stands
7. Vendors of religious oils, candles, and items

NOTE: It is essential for students to realize that many of the stands and stores in a other countries may be small in size. The traffic they attract and the business they receive is quite impressive. I was over-whelmed by the colors, scents and variety of tiny stands I found in the central plaza of Rio Piedras, Puerto Rico. I still carry these vivid images with me years after my trip to Puerto Rico. In one section of the marketplace, there were 20 - 30 tiny family restaurants serving food cafeteria style. The restaurants were only big enough to fit two cooks and their food offerings of the day. All customers sat outside in a plaza or courtyard.

Windows and Mirrors Follow-Up

- What do you see when you look at the slides of different markets?
- As you think about your own consumption, do you know where your fruit, drinks, and foods come from

before arriving in the produce section of your neighborhood grocery store?

- Imagine that you are a new citizen of the United States from a country where small farms and roadside vendors are the primary source of buying food. What would your reaction be to large scale grocery store chains?
- In large, densely populated cities like New York, it is still very common for people to take daily walks for fresh baked breads, fruits, and other groceries. How is city life different from smaller towns where there may be fewer choices available?
- How do you feel about the use of pesticides and chemicals to grow produce?
- If available in your town or city, are organic fruits and vegetables viable options for all people? Is affordability an issue?
- What is a food desert? Do you live in one?

ACTIVITY 16: SOLVING WORLD PROBLEMS – AMBASSADORS OF ALTRUISM

Staging: Computer, Poster, Markers, etc.

Goals: Developing an awareness of how Non-governmental organizations (NGOs) and globally focused organizations work to build a more sustainable world. Understanding the specific missions of powerful organizations like the United Nations.

Suggested Steps:

1. Research the mission statements of United Nations, UNESCO, World Health Organization and others.

2. Contrast the work of the UN or UNESCO with the purpose that embassies and consulates serve.
3. Explore the careers of people that serve as ambassadors, diplomats, and international delegates. Given that such a small percentage of the overall population works in international fields, seek to demystify these professional career pathways.
4. Ask students to focus on a part of the world and one specific country that interests them.
5. Revisit the United Nations SDGs outlined earlier in the book. Research the specific SDG that is most pressing in the country you chose.

Explore resources and research tools with your students including online databases, libraries, potential expert academicians at a nearby university, and consulate offices if one exists in your city. Prepare an official briefing note on your country as it relates to the SDG challenge it faces. The Internet is replete with guidelines on how to craft a briefing note, and I have included a few of the key features below:

- Try to limit your briefing note to page.
- State your case using only factual data formatted with bullet points.
- Scan the web for examples of actual briefing notes.
- Include basic metrics about the country that help to illustrate how the SDG applies.

Windows and Mirrors Follow-Up

- Reflect on your learning in this activity. Were you aware of the United Nations SDGs prior to this research?

- How does looking at a SDG challenge from a "window" perspective differ from seeing it from a "mirror" vantage point?

ACTIVITY 17: MEETING OF THE MINDS

Staging: A large room is needed for this simulation. If budget allows, consider providing snacks and other décor that make the event have a gala feel. Recruit volunteers to serve the role as service personnel for the mock event.

Goals: Gaining awareness of luminaries from other countries across varied sectors of business, academia, entertainment, and philanthropy. Researching the biographies of preeminent and influential people in other cultures.

Suggested Steps:

1. Describe the concept of a cultural luminary. How would one earn this status and repute?

2. Survey what students know about galas, professional conferences, and colloquiums.

3. This is a powerful, highly interactive simulation. I have used it successfully over the years in a variety of classroom and training contexts. The list of luminaries I have chosen below was for a training on Latin American, Spain, and Caribbean culture. Your lists are limited only by your imagination so tailor this to meet your needs.

3. Explain to participants that they are going to engage in "method acting" and assume to role of a luminary attending an influential "meeting of the minds" annual event. During the gala, they will rub elbows with other famous people from the Spanish-speaking world.

HISTORICAL FIGURES

- Judge Sonya Sotomayor, José Martí
- Juan Pablo Duarte, Evita Perón
- Ellen Ochoa, Dolores Huerta
- Cesar Chavez, Celia Cruz
- Tito Puente, Frida Kahlo
- Diego Rivera, Pablo Neruda
- Juan Luis Guerra, Isabel Allende
- Salvador Dalí, Ana María Matute
- Guillermo del Toro, Rigoberta Manchú
- Rafael Nadal, Antonia C. Novello

5. Participants should be given the ability to choose their character, time to research, and time to prepare for the role of a lifetime. Encourage them to read, view video clips, and learn as much as they can. Give them the date and time of the mock gala.

6. Each participant will arrive at the mock gala in the persona of the luminary. The gala does not require any special attire as the simulation is about substance and learning about the contributions and historical significance of everyone in attendance.

7. As facilitator and host, you may want to open with the following keynote welcome:

This is the last time today that I will speak to you as your facilitator/teacher. In a minute I will ask you all to leave the room. As soon as you exit, you will return to the room one by one. You must knock to gain admittance. Upon seeing me, your distinguished host, you should introduce yourself and shake my hand. When all of you enter the room, you are required to mingle and try to meet everyone present at the party. At no point should you form triads or small groups. You must connect with each person on a 1 to 1 level. The goal of your conversations is to learn everything you can about each of your fellow guests. Throughout the process, jot down notes so you can recall the names, biographical data, and histori-cal/ cultural significance of everyone. Every 5 minutes, you will hear a bell. This signifies that you should politely end the conversa-tion and move on to the next person you see. Enjoy the party.

8. Usher everyone out of the room and make your final prepara-tions. As each luminary returns to the room, greet them gregari-ously, and guide them into the event space. Along with your volunteers, monitor the event and constantly make the rounds to ensure that students are engaged for the entire time.

9. After about 30 - 45 minutes declare that the event has ended, and announce:

Thank you for attending this gala. Never again will such an amazing collection of individuals be gathered in one place. When you are ready to exit, please leave the room and reenter as the students in my class.

10. Participants reenter the room. Typically, there is substantial buzz about what just transpired. Your role is to facilitate a debriefing.

Windows and Mirrors

- How many of the celebrities in attendance had you heard of prior to the gala?
- What research might you continue to do about someone you met at the gala?
- What careers or categories of luminaries should have been represented?
- How does learning about others alter your thinking about the countries or cultures that were in attendance?

ACTIVITY 18: I'VE GOT THE MUSIC IN ME

Staging: Sound clips and excerpts from songs; lyric sheets to songs in a cloze activity format.

Goals: Cultural awareness regarding popular or folkloric musical forms from other countries. Amplification and enrichment of your musical culture knowledge. Connecting musical expression to certain cultural regions, eras in history, and to unique political, environmental, socio-economic, and humanitarian movements.

Suggested Steps:

1. Prompt discussion on what participants know about musical styles from around the world.

2. As you study different geographic regions or countries, incorporate listening experiences that focus on diverse musical expression. For example, when studying the Caribbean, include audio and video clips of merengue, salsa, bachata, bomba, Afro-Caribe jazz, etc.

3. Create a digital playlist of your songs from Spanish-speaking countries representing a variety of genres and sub-genres.

4. Consider designing some lyric sheet cloze activities for different songs. It helps to focus student attention and promotes great analysis of songs.

5. When teaching songs and genres, consider using a template to solicit reactions:

- This music reminds me of…
- Listening to this style of music makes me feel like…
- I hear the following instruments…
- This style of music is called…and it originated in…
- What are some other things that come to mind as I hear this music?

NOTE: I rarely ask participants to tell me whether they like a certain type of music or not. Peer pressure can often cloud or influence responses. I focus, instead, on discussion, learning to identify musical styles, and learning about the cultural context for different songs and styles.

Here are several Latino genres to explore with your students:

- Merengue
- Spanish Pop
- Onda Grupera
- Spanish Rap
- Son
- Lambada
- Salsa
- Ranchera
- Rumba
- Tango
- Latin Jazz
- Sonero
- Flamenco
- Afro-Caribe Jazz
- Compas
- Bomba
- Bachata
- Andean Folk
- Folkloric
- Baladas
- Cuatro
- Plena
- Boleros
- Pachanga
- Cumbia
- Protest – La Nova Trova
- Danzon

- Reggaeton
- Conjunto
- Forro
- Marimba
- Tejano
- Jibaro
- Mariachi
- Quechua
- Corrido
- Tuna
- Vallenato
- Bossa Nova

Mirrors and Windows:

- Are there benefits listening to music without understanding the lyrics?
- Are you aware of how certain sounds alter your emotional state?
- If every genre of music were a window into a culture, what assumptions would you make about anything you listened to during this exercise?

ACTIVITY 19: JOURNAL OF THE SAVVY TRAVELER— CULTURE LOGS

Staging: Journals or blogs.

Goals: Learning the art of journaling to log experiences and reflect. Explore how travel can have multiple layers of depth in terms of understanding another culture.

Suggested Steps:

1. Explore the concept of travel writing. Discuss the reasons why people keep journals or digital records of their travels and experiences. Posit the role of social media and social networks in sharing experiences.

2. Explain to participants that keeping a culture journal while traveling is an essential way to capture incidents and experiences as they happen. In an age of selfies and captions, there is little time to reflect on experience. The rush to make a post and see who views or likes it robs us of a deeper analysis.

3. You might want to introduce the journal concept in the following way:

> As you travel, you will encounter people, events, incidents that you find odd, curious, delightful, and maybe even disorienting. A traditional paper journal allows you the space to record initial thoughts and then revisit later in the day, week, etc. Taking photos with your phones only captures the image but doesn't get to the heart of how you felt or interpreted the subject. As travelers, your imagination, flexibility, intuition, and sense of adventure are essential. Your job is simple: learn how to be a savvy traveler and try to learn as much as you can. Seek to understand what you see and experience through your own words or use the journal to interview locals.

4. Practice some "savvy traveler" experiences by helping participants build a structure around their journal entries. One such format is listed below:

- **LOCATION**: Where were you when you saw this?
- **INCIDENT**: What happened? Try to describe without interpretation.
- **REACTION** to the experience: How did you react?

- **LOCAL EXPERTS**: Did you speak with anyone? Did you ask questions?

5. Participants are free to use whatever format may work for them. The essential lesson here is the art of slowing down and reflecting on experience. In a classroom setting, I would have a large collection of cultural artifacts, film clips, personal stories, case studies that easily lend themselves to a "savvy traveler" reflection. Here are some examples.

SPORTS

- Video of Jai Alai
- Video of Cricket
- Video of Curling

EVENTS AND TRADITIONS

- La Tomatina
- Semana Santa Processions
- Bull Fights
- Pilgrimages
- Día de los Muertos

ART

- Dalí
- Picasso
- Pollack
- Rivera
- Kahlo
- O'Keefe

CRAFTS

- Piñata
- Ojo del Diablo
- Weaving

Note: Again, these examples come directly from past high school Spanish classroom experiences, but you can alter the list and contents to represent any culture, region, and country you wish. The process is what matters as content is variable.

ACTIVITY 20: CHILDHOOD GAMES

Staging: Books or websites on authentic childhood games played in various parts of the world. Video clips or a slide deck of actual games being played or taught.

Goals: Global Awareness around the role of childhood games. Understanding the ways in which games are played in other cultures.

Suggested Steps:

1. Explore the concept of childhood games. Encourage students to share some of their favorite games. Record the generated list visually somewhere either in your room or on a device.

2. Discuss how games are effective ways to get to know people and their culture.

3. Ask participants to independently research a game played by children in another country or culture and investigate the following:

- Where is the game played?
- Who plays it?

- What are the rules of this game?
- What are its origins?

4. Have your students share the results of their search. Consider having each participant/researcher demonstrate how the game is played.

Windows and Mirrors Follow-Up

- Do you remember one of the games you played when you were younger?
- If you were visiting another country and saw this game being played in a park or school yard, what feelings might you feel?
- How has the notion of "play" changed as you have gotten older?
- What game from your childhood would you preserve for future generations? Why?

ACTIVITY 21: JOURNAL OF THE SAVVY TRAVELER – ENCOUNTERS AND INTERVIEWS

Staging: If in-person, consider a podium with participants seated in the round. If virtual, stage the Zoom (or other platform) so that you can control the use of audio and chat features. Savvy traveler journals.

Goals: Empathy building. Cultural understanding through dialogue and personal connection. Practicing the art of listening.

Suggested Steps:
1. Consider an online membership with an educational organi-

zation or partner school to facilitate dialogue with students from another country.

2. Invite a consul general or consulate staff member to visit your classroom.

3. Previous to any discussion, discuss the ways in which speakers are limited in representing their culture due to their own Windows and Mirrors perspectives.

4. Prepare a list of thoughtful questions that go beyond "surface culture." Here are some examples of student-generated questions:

1. Who are your country's national heroes?
2. What do the colors and symbols on your flag represent?
3. Do you have a national anthem? Does it commemorate a historical event? Does it celebrate places and people?
4. What does your national anthem sound like? Will you sing it for us?
5. Besides your native language, do you speak other languages?
6. What are the main religions in your country? Are people tolerant of each other's religious practices and beliefs?
7. What are some of the main challenges that teenagers face in your country?
8. What is the attitude toward divorce?
9. What are the most important holidays? What are the most popular?
10. Do you celebrate "All Saints Day"?
11. How is family defined? Are there all kinds of families? Is the family concept very important?
12. Do most people work 9 - 5 workdays? How much vacation leave do people have? What kinds of things do people do on vacation? Are there special places that people visit?
13. When are stores open? Are there large grocery stores? Are there small markets?

14. How do people spend their leisure time? What are the favorite recreational activities of people?

15. Do you have a national "pastime" or sport? What games do children like to play?

16. Do you have private schools? Do you have public or government/tax-funded schools? Describe a typical school day for students of different ages. What types of things are there for kids to do after school?

17. When can teenagers apply for a driver's license? Do they have to take a test?

18. Describe your criminal justice system. Are there jails? Are drugs legal? Do you have the death penalty?

19. Do most people own cars? Are there taxis? Do people ride bikes? How about motorcycles?

20. What kinds of public transportation exist?

21. Do many tourists visit your town or city? What are the most frequently visited places?

22. Do most people own a television? Do most people own computers? Is the Internet widespread? How about social networks?

23. What are the most popular types of music?

24. Do many people speak English? How would most people describe the U.S.A.?

25. What is the name of your money? Do you use bills or coins? Could you send us some samples?

26. How did your country get its name? How about your hometown?

27. How many meals a day do you eat? What are some of the foods that your country is famous for? Which meal is the largest meal?

28. Do many people have maids? Are there many poor people?

29. Do you get along with most countries? Do you have enemies? Has your country ever been in a war?

30. Is crime a problem?
31. Is education free? Do most people go to college?
32. Describe your political system. Do you hold elections?
33. What is the typical dress of women? Men? Teenage boys? Teenage girls?
34. What are the greatest challenges facing your country? Are people working together to solve the problems?
35. What attitudes exist about a green economy?
36. Are you dependent on foreign aid?
37. Do you import more than you export? What do you import? What do you export?
38. Which of the United Nations SDGs is in most urgent need of being addressed? Can you offer a solution to the challenge?

NOTE: This list, although quite extensive, barely scratches the surface of all the possible questions that can be asked.

Windows and Mirrors Follow-Up

- In thinking about the Windows and Mirrors construct for understanding cultures, would you classify each question asked of the visitor as a different window or was the person one window through which you solicited answers?
- If you were in the "hot seat" how would you have answered each of the questions? What questions would have been a struggle?

ACTIVITY 22: CONSULTING THE CONSULATES

Staging: Devices for email, stationery for snail mail.

Goals: Understanding the role of consuls general and consulate offices.

Suggested Steps:

1. Explore the role of international embassies and consuls general in international cities. Discuss the ways in which countries self-promote and encourage tourism. Ask students about their experiences writing formal letters.

2. Visit the websites of large cities with a significant international business presence. Download a listing of consulate offices and consuls general.

3. Students will conduct Internet research to find informative websites about the country's embassy and department of tourism. Students are expected to submit these sites to the class wiki or website. Over time, you will collectively compile a list and links to the various agencies and embassies.

Announce the following:

> Now that we have completed our research, we are going to write formal email requests to all the embassies of the countries we learned about. In your communications, be sure to include who you are, what we are studying, and what we are interested in learning. Ask each embassy to send us posters, brochures, video, digital files, or anything else that might help us learn more about their culture.

Windows and Mirrors Follow-Up

- How might a consul general see the issues facing his or her country differently than an ordinary citizen?
- Would you make an effective cultural ambassador for your country?

ACTIVITY 23: SHOW AND TELL

Staging: Provide a safe place for the display of participant artifacts and memorabilia from home.

Goals: Gain a better understanding of how your family's cultural history is represented in artifacts and heirlooms. Connect your discovery to a curiosity about learning the significance of items that others have from their cultures and histories.

Suggested Steps:

1. Converse with students about the tangible things they value. Explore the idea of nostalgia, symbolic value, and family heirlooms.

2. After your schema activation discussions, assign the following: Take a look around your home. Make note of the items and objects you own and collect. Try to identify one item that best represents your idea of U.S. culture or your family's cultural background

3. The following day students should bring their items to the classroom. This activity works best if you organize your desks into a circle. Have students take turns showing their object, explaining what it is and why it is important, and passing it around. You might want to have a scribe keep a written record of all the objects brought to class.

Windows and Mirrors Follow-Up

- How did your artifact represent you or your family history?
- Would you expect someone from a different culture to have the same kinds of artifacts and heirlooms in their homes? Why or why not?
- Do any of the items you have at home stir up emotional reactions? If possible, tell us about the item and why it engenders such feelings.

ACTIVITY 24: THE ARCHEOLOGICAL DIG

Staging: Access to a remote area on school grounds, a small shovel, ribbons,

Goals: Understanding the contributions of archeologists and anthropologists in the study of cultures.

Suggested Steps:

1. Discuss the work of an archaeologist. Consider inviting an archeologist from a local higher education institution to speak with the class and facilitate a Q and A.

2. Find a location on school grounds in which you could simulate an archaeological dig. Be sure to seek the permission and support of your school principal and maintenance department.

3. Mark off a very small area using stakes and ribbons. Before your students arrive, bury an object beneath a bed of leaves or shrubbery. REMEMBER: This is imaginary. You do not need to do any digging or strenuous work.

4. Design a simple map ahead of time and ask your students to escort you and the class to the official dig site. Teach a student the

meticulous processes involved in a safe dig. Watch as the student unearths the object.

A typical conversation with prompts might include:

Teacher: What did you find?

Student: It looks like a jar of some sort… no?

Teacher: Are jars usually made of this material?

Student: No way! Jars are not wooden.

Teacher: So, if it is not a jar, what else might it be?

Student: Can you put stuff in it? I mean, can it function like a jar?

Teacher: I would like everybody to take about five minutes to write down some ideas about the function of this object. Just take some guesses and don't worry about being right or wrong. We are all going to figure this out together.

After students have jotted down their thoughts, encourage them to share their conjectures with the class. Listen carefully to their answers but try not to reveal the true function of the object until you have completed the next step.

Repeat their answers aloud and have the class vote. Tell the students the real answer and make sure they write down the name of the object in their notes.

Windows and Mirrors Follow-Up

- If you could only choose one career, would you prefer that of an archeologist or anthropologist? Explain your thinking.
- Would you expect someone from a different culture to have the same kinds of artifacts to exhume if a similar exercise was done? Why or why not?

- What remnants would you leave behind for someone to find 60, 70, or 80 years into the future? What assumptions would a future archeological team make about you and how you lived?
- Have you ever visited a Natural History Museum and looked at any of the installations that exhibit artifacts exhumed by archeologists? What judgments did you make about those cultures on display?

ACTIVITY 25: CELEBRATIONS AND HOLIDAYS

Staging: Calendars from other countries.

Goals: Global Awareness. Understanding the holidays celebrated in other countries and the meanings behind them.

Suggested Steps:

1. Ask participants to brainstorm different categories and kinds of holidays: federal government, religious, historical, and cultural.

2. Facilitate a discussion about the origins of holidays and the ways in which cultures celebrate different days.

3. This experience describes an activity I designed with Maria Elena Juan at the National Endowment of Humanities Institute at the University of Puerto Rico. This is one example of how a holiday can be experienced in a classroom setting. The topic is the "Día del Santo" or "Saint's Day" as it is celebrated in many parts of Spain. The information below reflects the experience of one citizen of Spain. Please keep this in mind as you read. I think it is incumbent upon us as teachers to use great caution when presenting cultural phenomena or norms to our students.

It is always advisable to consult native speakers for our research. In addition, it is prudent to preface any discussion or description of cultural behaviors by using the following phrases:

"For some people…
"According to native speakers I spoke to…"
"Based on my own experience…"

For example, use the following information to help students understand the concept of Saint's Day as celebrated in most parts of Spain.

- Saint's Day is a religious holiday rooted in Roman Catholic tradition.
- Most Catholic children have names that are derived from the names of a saint.
- Saint's Day is celebrated much like a birthday in that a child receives cake, candy and many congratulations.
- Typically, a gift is not given on Saint's Day but on a child's birthday.
- Both Saint's Day and birthdays are celebrated.

4. Once students understand the concept, it is helpful to use a Venn diagram or other graphic to contrast a birthday celebration in the United States with a child's Saint's Day celebration in parts of Spain.

5. Repeat this activity by having students choose a holiday from their own upbringing. Consider having each student research a holiday from another country using the same template above from Saint's Day in Spain.

Other Holiday Celebrations to Explore:

- Diwali
- Hanukkah
- Chinese New Year
- Ramadan and Eid al-Fitr
- Boxing Day

- Día de los Muertos
- Kwanzaa

Note: This is just a sampling. Add your own.

Windows and Mirrors Follow-Up

- What holidays were celebrated in your family?
- What holidays were not celebrated in your family?
- Do you associate certain holidays with specific emotions or feelings?
- Are you aware of a holiday celebrated by other cultures and countries? If yes, how did you learn about it?

ACTIVITY 26: GESTURES

Staging: Excerpts from Gestures: The DO's and TABOOS of Body Language Around the World (see reference below).

Goals: Heightened cultural understanding about gestures, non-verbal language, and histrionics.

Suggested Steps

1. Explore the concept of nonverbal communications with students. Ask students to think of ways they use gestures to communicate meaning or emotion. Explain the concept of histrionics.

2. Ask volunteers to demonstrate a gesture. Discuss the connection between the gesture and its actual meaning. Is there a logic to it?

3. There are several excellent books written about intercultural communication and the use of gestures. For example, Roger E. Axtell's 1998 text, *Gestures: The DO's and TABOOS of Body Language*

Around the World published by Jon Wiley & Sons, Inc. Using Axtell's book as a guide, share some of his most intriguing gestures with your students.

4. Encourage student volunteers to guess the meanings of the different gestures you present.

5. Share personal stories from your own travels that are particularly illustrative. Ask students to do the same.

6. Design experiential activities incorporating gestures. For example,

- Conduct a session of your class using only nonverbal communication. Process the experience with students and discuss their frustration or enjoyment of the exercise.
- Play a few rounds of gesture bingo with all the gestures you have learned in class throughout the year. Ask students to customize an empty bingo grid (see https://teachlearnlead.net/) by writing the meaning of a specific (and different) gesture in each available space on the grid. As the facilitator utilizes a gesture, students check off the corresponding space where the meaning is written. This entire activity can be done in complete silence.

Windows and Mirrors Follow-Up

- Do you use gestures? When? Why?
- If you were traveling abroad, would you take the time to learn about country- or culture-specific gestures or would you just wing it and learn as you go?
- Are there certain gestures that you feel are more powerful than the equivalent word or expression could ever be?

CHAPTER 5

DESIGNING SOCIAL IMPACT AND SERVICE-LEARNING EXPERIENCES

Everyone must decide whether he will walk in the light of creative altruism or in the darkness of destructive selfishness.

MARTIN LUTHER KING, JR.

Kayla was a timid, unassuming student with a moderate interest in athletics and the arts. Yet, when she spoke of her love for livestock and sustainability, an ecstatic, engaged teen emerged. "I want to start a mini farm on our school's campus so that future students can learn to steward long after I graduate. We will grow food for the dining hall. Oh, and I want chickens too!" Her passion was palpable. As the president of the school at the time, it was both my practice and my passion to explore openly with students their ideas and motivation for pursuing passion projects. In this case, I stood at the cliff of either feeding her dreams or diverting them. There was no true middle ground for me as one who preaches a belief in the power of kids to bring compelling and affirming ideas to any table. I challenged Kayla to submit a multi-year vision for the unused, dilapidated greenhouse on campus. In under 48 hours, she returned to pitch her idea to a room full of astonished faculty.

Fast forward 3 months from that initial meeting and a verdant parcel of our school's 24 acres is now dedicated to what we have lovingly named the "Homestead": a working greenhouse, a student-built chicken coop, composting and vermiculture stations, a pollinator garden, and community partnership grants for a trout hatchery and apiary. Whole Foods Foundation recognized us with $6,000 in grant money and a once unsure student now makes the connection between passion, vision, and action. Simply stated, all students are capable of transformational change in this world. That first seed Kayla planted into our school's ethos and terrain has blossomed beyond any measure.

Social impact and service-learning are the ideal inside/out experiences for transforming and understanding cultures. This final chapter is dedicated to the topic, and I hope that you will consider designing similar experiences for your students. Having lived internationally at a young age, I learned the value of seeing the world and experiencing its uniqueness through the eyes of those who are natives of cultures other than my own. At that stage in my career, I was a strong proponent and practitioner of experiential-based learning and teaching. In the winter of 1996, my life and world view were radically altered while working as a world language and culture teacher at Northfield Mount Hermon School in Massachusetts. I was approached by my supervisor and asked to lead a group of 10 students for a 3-month educational and youth internship trip to the Dominican Republic.

The goals of the trip were multi-faceted. First, my students were expected to learn Dominican culture through homestays and language immersion. This objective was met quite readily through daily class sessions, family relationships, and practice with the language in authentic and challenging contexts. Second, each student was expected to serve the people in the local community of San

Cristobal. This was accomplished by a 3-month internship program. Each student decided on a social service that interested them. At that point, we identified places in the community that were welcoming to young interns. The jobs they held varied greatly along the service continuum. To illustrate, several students volunteered in local hospitals while others worked in elementary schools and orphanages. The experience was trajectory shifting on many levels for all of us.

As a result of my 1996 experience, I maintained a close relationship with the same family of orphanages on the island and committed to continuing the program with any new schools that I worked. From 1996 – 2016, I kept that promise and designed similar experiential programs for Episcopal High School of Jacksonville, Florida and The Bement School in Deerfield, Massachusetts. In the case of Bement, the trip was fully supported by a visionary school head and faculty and became a mandatory capstone experience for our graduating 9th grade class. The Dominican Orphanage project was a success in many ways. I kept my pledge to the orphanage and established a long-term relationship across three generations of orphanage leadership. In total, we were able to bring hundreds of students and faculty to live in and work in an orphanage and to make a lasting. The library we created, the school we worked on, and the infrastructure still remain. More importantly, the lives that were changed in both countries through friendship and cooperation have endured.

In the early years, as amazing as these expeditions were, I had always felt that the one piece they lacked was a stronger educational and cross-cultural training dimension to supplement the experiential component. The real learning happened in living off the grid. Most of our students had never been without technology, iPhone service, hot water, reliable plumbing, and electricity. This program demanded students to live orphanage culture from the inside/out even if just for a matter of weeks. The objective I had was to build empathy in our kids, create bridges of friendship between many different cultures, and to collaborate with the orphanage on service projects that they specifically chose.

SERVICE-LEARNING BACKGROUND

The most impactful service-learning initiatives are purposeful and integrated on a continuing basis as part of a school's or organization's curriculum. Over the past two decades, many middle and secondary schools have revamped and tweaked aspects of their curriculum to allow students opportunities to engage in meaningful service-learning. Roberts, in her book (p.4) Kids Taking Action, cites a U.S. Department of Education survey indicating that an estimated thirty-eight percent of middle schools in the nation had students participating in service-learning. There are numerous reasons that schools have led the way in the inclusion of service-learning:

1. Higher education has flipped the paradigm and minimized (in many cases eliminated) the need or over-reliance of standardized test scores as a predictor for future student success. Qualitative and soft skills are now key differentiators in applications. Often, this includes measures of student integrity, character, resolve, and ingenuity in the form of past service-learning or social entrepreneurship experiences.
2. As social problems like poverty, polarization, climate change, and crime, etc., continue to be prevalently featured in the news headlines, more and more teachers see the value in trying to develop skills in students that empower them to be future leaders and problem solvers.
3. The United Nations 17 Sustainable Development Goals (SDGs) have sounded the clarion call for all nations to make significant change globally by 2030. The clock is

ticking on these enormously important goals as I publish this book in the summer of 2023.

4. As the mental health epidemic has catapulted itself into the everyday discussions of media, health organizations, schools, churches, and policy makers, there is research-based evidence that service to others – domestically and internationally – can serve as an elixir to uplift spirits and embolden a self-worth.

5. In her groundbreaking research, Billig (2002) argues that the impacts for service-learning are numerous including personal and social development of youth, increased understanding of civic responsibility, enhanced academic learning, career exploration and aspirations, and positive influence on school and larger community. Billig reported that "students who engaged in service-learning were more likely to treat one another kindly, help one another, and care about doing their best." These results are all building blocks to creating a better world.

Many educators assert that a positive experience with service-learning can, in the words of Halstad (2002), "add to a student's self-knowledge and accomplishments precisely at the tender age when they are trying to find out who they are…and what they can offer the world. Addison and Addison-Jacobsen (1995) identified six groups that benefited because of their service-learning projects:

- Students
- Beneficiaries of the service
- The school as an institution
- The community at large
- Teachers
- Administrators

LEARNING GOALS/OUTCOMES

Shifting back to my work in intercultural understanding and partnerships across 20 years in the Dominican Republic, there are several learning objectives that are essential in a backwards design of a social impact and service-learning experience. I would like all my students and staff to return from our trek having made significant gains in the following areas:

1. **Intercultural Understanding** – Plain and simple, we build bridges when we make meaningful connections with others. The most meaningful and enduring form that cultural understanding takes is when it occurs in a natural context and free of the confining walls of a classroom.

2. **Empathy** – Students that participate in the trip to the Dominican Republic learn empathy and develop an increased understanding of the lives of abandoned youth. In addition, they are forced to step out of their own comfort zones and into a world that is completely alien to them.

3. **Historical Knowledge** – Typically, the trip has focused mainly on goodwill work and interactions with the children of the orphanage. Despite attempts to develop a pre-trip orientation program to learn about Dominican history and culture, the gains I wish to see in cultural/historical literacy of participants has yet to be realized in any significant ways. This is a work in progress.

4. **Geographical Knowledge** – Students that participate on this trip had a very limited sense of the geography of the Dominican Republic before visiting. This is a larger issue in U.S. schools and one worth addressing in positive ways.

5. **Socio-economic Knowledge** – What are the main challenges a country or city or community faces in its own sustainability? What are the business models that tend to thrive? How is the country performing if we were to rate it using the United Nations SDGs as benchmarks?

6. **Philanthropic and Social Entrepreneurial Understanding** – Upon completing this trip, I would hope that students experience and voice a desire to learn more about philanthropy and service as a field or career. Throughout our time on the island, we debrief and process what we see and learn. Inevitably, the questions, "What can be done to help these kids after we leave?" and "What agencies exist to work with orphanages worldwide?" emerge in our discourse. It would be an ideal learning outcome if students can gain some philanthropic sensibilities as a result of this program.

7. **Self-Discovery** – Throughout the entire 7 - 8 days we travel, our students experience many levels of adversity and challenge. Among the most common experiences are issues around guilt, privilege, homesickness, and culture shock. My hope is that students approach the trek as an opportunity for self-discovery.

DESIGN AND DEFINE

There are endless ways to approach the architectural design of social impact and service-learning experiences. The most important component, however, is being clear and authentic about the purpose. On the previous page, I outlined my six primary goals and learning outcomes: *intercultural understanding, empathy, historical knowledge, geographical knowledge, philanthropic cultivation, socio-economic knowledge, and self-discovery.*

In terms of specific program design features that integrate the goals, schedules, service projects, and impact, there are five essential elements

1. **Pre-Trip** – Will there be fundraising component to support the program and invest in the orphanage? What is the budget? What are the behavioral and medical policies, waivers, and legal considerations? How will we design a comprehensive **orientation** including several sessions to outline the mission and purpose of the trip, learn key language expressions, cultural norms, non-verbal expressions, and semiotics. What goodwill gift will we bring to the orphanage?

2. **Orphanage Primer** – Very few of our participants have any inside understanding of the nature of orphanage life. How did the orphanage start? How is it funded? Who does it serve? Who has access? Who are the kids we will meet? What is our objective while there? What specific projects have we been asked to accomplish?

3. **Experiential Underpinnings** - In the spirit of John Dewey and Kurt Lewin, how will the experiential design of the program incorporate daily individual and group reflections?

4. **In-Country Programmatic Systems** – What are the channels for regular check-ins with trip leaders? The orphanage staff? Participants and their families back home? What is the workflow and system of deliverables on projects? How do we structure the difficult goodbyes? How will we plan a meaningful celebration? How do we memorialize our time together for both the orphanage and our participants? (Example: a collaborative mural with a year time stamp)

5. **Post-trip & Reentry**- How do we debrief and process the experience with each other, the families, and the school? What kinds of presentations can we do to share with our

communities? How will we maintain communication and continuity?

PRE-TRIP - GENERATIVE TOPICS

Staging: This orientation period pre-trip is extensive and extends multiple weeks. A consistent classroom space or venue would be ideal.

Goals: Build working knowledge of the orphanage, behavioral expectations, intercultural understanding challenges. Teach basic language expressions.

Suggested Steps:

In designing a series of activities for a pre-trip, multi-week orientation, it is important to identify additional parameters for students and the curriculum.

Here's what I communicated about a trip I took with some students:

The pre-trip work will take place for our entire 9th grade class (N=35) that is taking the journey together in February. While we will aim to be interdisciplinary in our approach and involve as many 9th grade teachers as possible, this is not always possible. The trip is led by me and our team of 9th grade advisors.

Our pre-trip activities are limited to a 1.5-hour block of time on Fridays (and occasionally 20–25-minute blocks of early morning time on Mondays, Wednesdays, and Thursdays) referred to as "Advisor Time." There is no expectation that other 9th grade teachers (math, science, history) will devote class time to the trip. This is the case for several reasons. First, not all 9th grade teachers make the trip and thus do not have any background for teaching about the Dominican Republic or the orphanage. Second, all planning, goals, and curriculum for the trip falls into the capable hands of the advisors and me.

The trip, although a capstone experience for our 9th grade students, is only one of many obligations they have during their final year at Bement (we are a K-9 junior boarding school). There are numerous other issues tugging at them including academic classes, athletic team commitments, and the daunting secondary school selection process that ensures their admission to a school for 10th grade year.

As Wiske stated, (p. 27) "choosing the topics students will study and deciding how to organize curriculum plans are some of the most difficult decisions a teacher makes." In planning a pre-trip unit on the Dominican Republic, there are myriad directions one can point. Do I focus on learning primarily about the country? Do I concentrate on orphanages and what it means to be an orphan? Do we immerse ourselves in the Dominican form of the Spanish language? Do we take a broader vision and delve into what it means to serve others and why an ethic of altruism is important? Wiske's table (p.28) of features was helpful in identifying answers to these questions.

ACTIVITY 27: PRE-TRIP-BUILDING A KNOWLEDGE BASE - PERSPECTIVES AND MISCONCEPTIONS

Staging: This orientation period pre-trip is extensive and extends multiple weeks. A consistent classroom space or venue would be ideal.

Goals: Build working knowledge of the orphanage, behavioral expectations, intercultural understanding challenges. Teach basic language expressions.

Suggested Steps:

Ideally, the pre-trip design would utilize a Learning by Design (LBD) approach to knowledge acquisition. By using the concept of generative topics and constructivist pedagogy, I would gather all students together to solicit several things from them. Privately, I would ask them to submit a list of all the things they are (a) curious about regarding the Dominican Republic and (b) a list of things they are feeling anxious or excited about regarding leaving the United States and doing experiential field work. In addition to privately sharing, I would also encourage students to articulate some of the things they wish to learn with the group present.

Ultimately, my goal is to have the students individually construct information based on the aspects of the Dominican Republic that interest them the most. Google Docs or similar collaborative platforms would serve as the orientation's online community hub. Shared documents provide myriad templates for grids and charts. As students post queries, research data, and share facts about the Dominican Republic, they would be invited to share their knowledge with their fellow travelers. I have included a sample chart on the next page to illustrate the kinds of topics and information that could be shared far in advance of the trip. This also allows participants to be active in building a collective knowledge base.

Queries and Research Topics	Quantitative and qualitative responses.	CITATIONS & RESOURCES
What is the main project we will be working on? Can we do more than one project?		
-What are some of the most popular musical genres and styles of the Dominican Republic?	-Merengue and bachata will be heard everywhere we travel on the island.	Research the history of these music forms and survey the genre's most famous artists. >Juan Luis Guerra
What is the current population of the island and other census statistics that may be of interest?		
What is the history of the orphanage? Who owns it? How many kids live there? How do they come to the orphanage?		
What are some topographical and geographical features of the Dominican Republic?		
Are there any current political or social issues in Dominican culture that we should be aware of?		
Other…		
Other…		

Again, in constructivist pedagogy tradition, it is essential to have student participants take full ownership of the knowledge base. These questions, while monitored by a teacher or group leader, are all generated by students. Every entry must be initialed by a student author and any facts presented should be accompanied by a citation. In addition, new rows and headings may be added at any time. This chart will be maintained throughout the year.

As students will utilize the Internet for much of their information gathering for this activity, I plan to teach a session on verifying web sources. This mini workshop will incorporate search exercises from chapters 3 and 5 in Alan November's <u>Web Literacy for Educators</u> book. These activities inspire critical thinking by introducing students to skills that help them to verify websites for accurate information. Jonassen's (p.30) recommendation of Zotero might also be a useful tool to model for students. The final column "citations and resources" of the grid will provide practice for students in learning how to properly cite their references.

ACTIVITY 28: PRE-TRIP TECHNOLOGY ENHANCED LEARNING AND VIRTUAL AGENTS

Staging: Device and IT expertise are needed for this activity.

Goals: Build student engagement across different platforms to enhance learning and interest.

Suggested Steps:

In a recent course at Columbia University Teachers College, Cognition and Computers, I researched the use of virtual agents and augmented reality as methods for engaging students and promoting more intrinsically motivated learning. Although hypothetical, the following activity incorporates some of that research and represents an ideal follow-up to the pre-trip activity.

Students would be introduced to several pedagogical agents (Graesser, 2008) in a computer program called Dominican Republic E-Tours. The virtual tutors or single agents would embody (Graesser, p.299) "individuals with different knowledge, personalities, physical features, and styles." In the case of Dominican Republic E-Tours, each agent would be a native Dominican and replicate Dominican linguistic patterns and vocabulary, idioms, and slang that is prevalent in (and unique to) the Dominican Republic.

Students could choose one of several agents based on preferences they have for agents of a certain gender or age. In addition, given that all software is identical, there is no advantage to choosing one agent over another. This part of the program is mainly designed for constructing preliminary knowledge of the country, history, and culture. Based on where the conversation goes with a respective agent, a student will be connected to video snippets or photographs depicting different cultural icons, sights, etc. For example, if a student inquires about Dominican cuisine, the agent can answer basic questions and link students to sites where he or she can learn more. Here is a sample interaction between agent and student:

> **AGENT/TUTOR (Sergio):** I am excited that you want to learn about my country. I'm Sergio. If you need any help with pronunciation along the way, simply click on any word written in Spanish and you will hear me pronounce it for you. So, where would you like to start your journey? What interests you most about my homeland?
>
> **STUDENT:** I used to live in New York and used to pass by many Dominican restaurants. I always wanted to try the food. What can you tell me about it?
>
> **AGENT/TUTOR (Sergio):** Food is always a popular topic. What food groups interest you the most? Look at the categories on the screen and select one that you want to learn about.
>
> **STUDENT:** Cool! There are some great choices. I'll probably explore them all, but let's start with the menu that explains staples.
>
> **AGENT/TUTOR (Sergio):** Well, as you can see, rice and beans are an important part of
>
> Dominican gastronomy. Why not select a dish from the pictures below and I'll connect you with an actual video of my aunt preparing the dish?

At this point, the student begins his in-depth exploration of Dominican food. There are more choices and videos to view in this category than a student has time to explore. While student A is learning about food, student B may be with a completely different agent learning about Dominican music and dance. The topics are endless. Student intrinsic motivation is very high at this point as all learning is tied directly to student interest.

ACTIVITY 29: IN-COUNTRY – DOCUMENTING THE JOURNEY

Staging: Discuss the platform that is most suitable for this kind of endeavor. Logistics and ethical considerations are essential to build consensus around as this trip is meant to be fully unplugged.

Goals: Provide a means of communication back home on a scheduled basis so that families and the school can support our efforts and learn of our progress. Creating a travel log for the creation of a time capsule post-trip so that all participants can forever be linked across the passage of time to the experience.

Suggested Steps:

Although access to the Internet is sketchy and sporadic, there are several internet café sites that would enable us to utilize communication platforms during the in-country portion of the trip. The main goal of such an activity would be to increase communication between participants in the program (students, group leaders) and our constituents/followers (parents, school community, media outlets) back in the United States.

Ideally, a podcast would be a wonderful way to communicate with our constituents, but while in-country we lack the materials and tools necessary to make this happen effectively. Two excellent alternatives would be the use of a photo-sharing account. First, our students take thousands of photos while in the Dominican Republic. In our daily morning meetings, we could decide collectively how to organize the photos we take. A different group of students would accompany a trip leader to an internet café each day of our stay and upload the photos with various captions, tags, or themes.

In terms of an audio/video production platform, the intent would be a bit different. Again, a different set of students could be tasked with telling the story of the orphanage through different kinds of media other than photographs. This footage could be used for orientations of future trips and also to fundraise for the orphanage. By showing the needs the orphanage has for supplies and the kinds of construction projects they would like to see completed in future years, there is opportunity for increased philanthropic support.

ACTIVITY 30: IN-COUNTRY REFLECTIONS

Staging: Any site on orphanage grounds that allows for a private meeting spot. Our meetings were always conducted in circle formation under the moonlight after all the children of the orphanage were sleeping. The designation of an object that can be passed around and signifies who is speaking. Research the "talking stick" concept if you are unfamiliar with this methodology.

Goals: Provide a regular debrief and processing of the intensity of the day's events. Encourage self-expression and honest feedback. Discussion of cultural norms and behaviors that were observed. Preview of the coming day.

Suggested Steps:

1. Gather all participants. Aim to make this reflection the same time every night. Review ground rules e.g. respecting one another and remaining silent and supportive when someone shares.

2. Ask a different student to bring his or her version of the nightly "talking stick."
3. The reflection begins with the first student's comment and then moves around the circle as the next person is ready to share

The following excerpts are samples of two reflections:

[Student #1] "These boys are all here for reasons. Their mothers, fathers, grandparents are gone or unable to take care of them. Thankfully though, these kids have been given a second chance. They are given a roof over their heads and food in their stomachs… happiness comes with life's simple things. These boys amazed me both times I have been lucky enough to see them. Every person who walks through the gate falls in love with their smiles and laughter. The boys all have a gift because each day they seem to live their lives to the fullest. Going to the Dominican Republic opened my eyes and taught me so many life lessons."

[Student #2] "That night, our entire group gathered on the roof of the orphanage for a nightly reflection circle. I remembered constantly passing tissues around the circle, as classmates felt over-whelmed by the ability of these boys who had so little, to love us so much. This time, we laugh together about the three-year-olds who try to kiss us goodnight. And through this laughter on the roof top, morning trips to visit an elementary school, and afternoon English lessons for the older boys, our group bonded. We only could have come together in the Dominican. There is something special in the purified water there; conversations are deeper, horizons are widened, friendships are made, and while saying goodbye is hard, I learned that week to live in the moment. For one week, grades, friends, classes, skating, and track did not matter. My needs did not even matter. Instead, I spent a week making other people smile."

ACTIVITY 31: POST-TRIP – SHARING WITH THE COMMUNITY

Staging: Find an appropriate venue for the group to present about the trip. Enlist IT support to share a slide deck and a sound system for student speakers.

Goals: Student public speaking and self-expression. Sharing of cultural learnings and details of the project.

Suggested Steps:

- Consider the audience. Who will you be presenting to?
- Consider the purpose. What is it that you want to convey? What will be your main area of focus?
- Consider the impact. Will you ask participants to make impact statements?
- What kinds of visuals will you use to help the audience connect to your trip on an emotional level?
- Will you invite members of the outside community? Supporters of the program who may have contributed to your fundraising events? The local media?
- What final message do you want to give the audience? Will there be a call to action?

ACTIVITY 32: POST-TRIP -ORPHANS AND ORPHANAGES

Staging: Classroom or venue for private discussion and debriefing.

Goals: Understanding the intensity of our experience. Treating reentry as an important component of closure. Final reflections on the orphanage and the children we met. Discussion of future action steps we might take as individuals and collectively to stay connected to the children we met at the orphanage.

Suggested Steps:

One of the most salient features of a trip such as this is the motivation students possess to do something concrete with their newfound knowledge. Upon returning to the United States, I am constantly exploring the student generated query, "What now? What more can we do to help the boys in the orphanage?" In this exercise, we spent several class periods learning about orphanages worldwide and the organizations that are involved in philanthropic and humanitarian work. We also visited the iEARN (Wiske, p.102 and Jonassen, p.p. 141-143) website and pored through hundreds of projects involving orphanage work.

I led students through a process of distilling down to a handful of schools whose projects match our interests. Students were genuinely surprised to see the large numbers of students participating in meaningful projects worldwide. In addition, they were delighted to learn about a group of high school students in Argentina doing similar work in the Dominican Republic. Our discovery led us to scheduling a series of real time discussions with the Argentinian students using web conferencing software (Jonassen, p. 112).

A few 9th graders expressed the importance of learning more about agencies that work with orphans in our local and state community. As a result, we designed an activity in which we generated a series of questions for the experts. I arranged a series of field trips for our students to tour local agencies, but this was not logistically possible for the state agencies. In this case, we worked with IVC (Jonassen, p. 112) technology and arranged interviews and discussions with experts that could not make the trip to our school. As Jonassen noted, "Videoconferencing overcomes barriers of cost and distance since physically transporting a classroom of students to another location is often impossible."

MOTIVATING STUDENT LEARNING – FANTASY, CHALLENGE, AND CURIOSITY

Malone (1981) argues that fantasy, challenge, and curiosity are all essential components of intrinsically motivating learning. The activities I have devised strive to encompass all these features. Student collaboration in the pre-activities serves to whet their curious appetites for knowledge vis a vis free choice explorations of any aspect of Dominican culture that interests them. Likewise, with the use of virtual agents in pre-activity #2, fantasy is addressed in an ongoing way using an agent/tutor that accompanies students on their virtual pre-trip treks.

Challenges exist at all levels of the activities. First, in the pre-activities there is a self-challenge to learn as much as possible about the Dominican Republic and an expectation that each student will contribute to our public knowledge base using Google Docs. Second, in both in-country and post-trip activities, students must rise to the respective challenges of (a) finding ways to voice and share their experiences with various audiences throughout our school including other students, parent groups, and faculty and (b) finding ways to continue the meaningful work they did at the orphanage.

Our students have made very personal connections with the orphans they lived with and often return with a burning desire to help them. Herein lies the philanthropic dimension of what they learn. The challenge is to use their knowledge and to share the stories of the Dominican boys with the community. Students realize that the more knowledgeable they are, and the better they can communicate, the greater the likelihood that they will be able to raise funds to help.

Finally, challenges that impact intrinsic motivation emerge in several other forms. Although we only spend a week on the island, we experience life as the orphans live it each day. Experiential learning demands full participation and immersion from the learner and is multilayered in terms of challenges. To illustrate, here are the most common types of adversity/ challenge that our students face:

Language – Most of our students are monolingual and/or only have very basic Spanish skills. Their inability to communicate verbally can be a source of frustration.

Culture Shock – Not only do students sign on to live in a different culture, but they are also immersed in a working orphanage. While in the country, they try to make sense of the things they see and experience. Culture shock (Furnham, 1993) is processed through group interaction, reflection, and debriefing. Students adapt quickly to the incessant ebb and flow of electricity, lack of hot water (or any water), sanitation issues, and the unfamiliar tastes and textures of food.

Homesickness- Many students have not traveled outside of their home country and, if they did, it was likely with their families. The experience of living in an orphanage – even for a short time – can weigh on one physically and emotionally. These feelings often manifest as intense homesickness.

An Unplugged Existence – Students and trip leaders sign a pledge to live a completely unwired existence throughout all phases of the trip. Students learn to live without their cell phones, iPads, and mobile devices. Their sole connections are face-to-face in real-time for the duration of the trip.

Wrestling with One's Own Privilege – Most of the participants I have taken on these experiential service trips are not quite prepared for some of the feelings that may emerge. First, seeing and living abject poverty up close, even for a short period of time, is often very difficult for participants to process. In stark contrast to the orphanage population served in developing nations, most of our students come from stable, loving homes, and enjoy the benefits that middle- to upper-level socioeconomic lifestyles afford. Students are challenged intellectually, ethically, and morally throughout this trip as they struggle to make sense of a world where the have and have-not scenario is visceral and ubiquitous. The most common patterns I have seen over the decades have been participants voicing anger toward a world that should be doing more to help and feeling guilty about recognizing their own privilege. Helplessness is often expressed as well but this feeling tends to dissipate amongst participants once the daily work starts and connections are made with the orphans.

CHAPTER 6
RESOURCES

There are an abundance of resources on global education, service-learning, and cultural understanding available to all of us. Amazing websites, organizations, NGOs, and apps are birthed incessantly. In 2014, my initially self-serving desire to have every possible resource at my fingertips, and accessible by a single click, inspired me to design the first prototype of the www.teachlearn-lead.net platform. Over time, this personal website became something I started to share within my school and then across the entire Internet. The vision for this passion project was to create a true, curated epicenter of resource-rich collections of links to K-20 research, educational topics, school design, global education, STEAM, and professional development resources. Some ten years later, teachlearnlead.net has become a thought leadership platform and an ongoing resource for teachers, educational leaders, and nonprofits across the globe.

In addition to the online platform, I have also included a few key resources for you here that were either mentioned in the book or inspired me in some way.

WEBSITES

- World Learning at https://www.worldlearning.org/
- The Experiment in International Living at https://www.experiment.org/
- SIT Graduate Institute at https://graduate.sit.edu/
- The Peace Corps at https://www.peacecorps.gov/
- United Nations at https://www.un.org/en/
- UNESCO at https://www.unesco.org/en
- Global Cognition at https://www.globalcognition.org/
- Center for Global Awareness at http://global-awareness.org/
- National Youth Leadership Council at https://nylc.org/
- SEITAR USA at https://www.sietarusa.org/
- IIE at https://www.iie.org/
- 4-H at https://4-h.org/
- Junior Achievement USA at https://jausa.ja.org/
- The International Social Impact Institute at https://internationalsocialimpactinstitute.com/

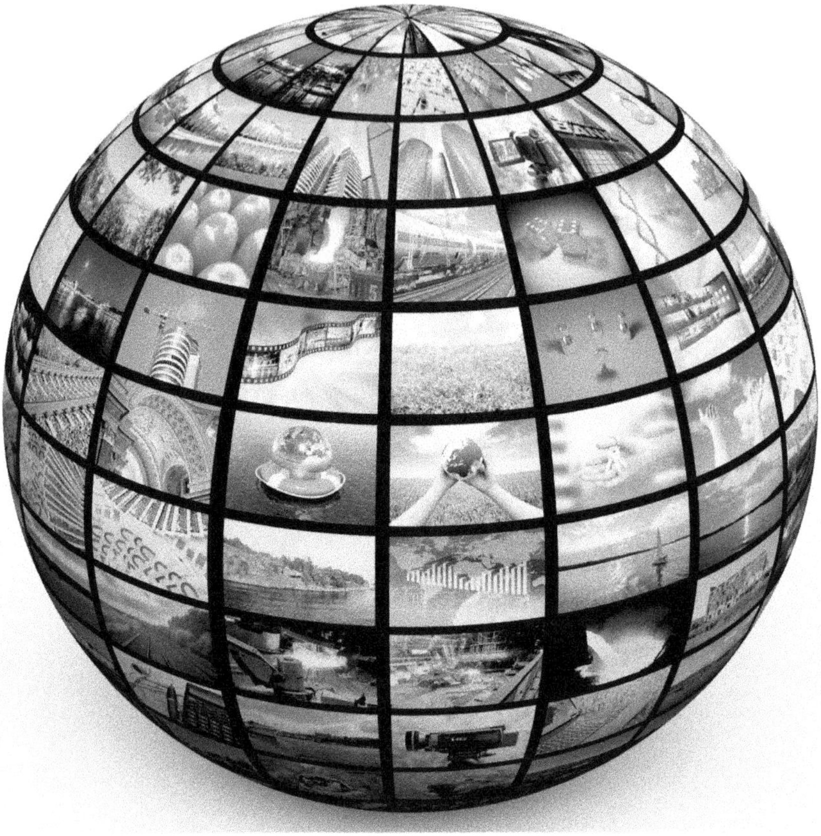

CONCLUSION

Your mind is a garden, thoughts are the seeds. You can grow
flowers, or you can grow weeds

OSHO

I was thinking a bit on the span of my lifetime to date and was hard
pressed to remember any period where our world was completely
at peace. From wars to terrorist attacks to mass shootings, it all just
seems to be part of our life on the planet. Yet, there is some well-
spring that replenishes me when I think about the individual
people I meet who are true changemakers. Every day, individuals
make choices to financially support their favorite charities, art institutions, churches, and non-profits. Others express their desire to
give through action. I meet volunteers of local soup kitchens, shelters, libraries, and hospitals. The Christophers claim a powerful
mantra, "better to light one candle than to curse the darkness!"

   The collective purpose of the activities, simulations, and experiences in Windows and Mirrors is to amplify our worldviews a bit
and develop both a stronger sense of self and a greater degree of

empathy and understanding for others. The lens I use is cultural understanding as my life has been transformed time and time again by travel and crossing cultures. When I began designing domestic and international service-learning programs in 2000, it was always with the hope that by serving others my students would grow into a life in which they recognized their ability to make a positive impact. This was the impetus, too, for my work in establishing immersive camps and programs in youth leadership and social entrepreneurship. Teaching these skills and habits is my way of infusing light into the hearts and minds of others. The light is no ordinary one because it has stayed with me decades after my first forays into a service-based life.

My hope is that soon you have the chance to experience some of these activities either in a classroom context, solo journaling, volunteering, or as a trainer. Their power comes from being lived and grappled with in whatever the chosen context and they are worth the time and energy needed to implement. I welcome your constructive feedback about how you used or tweaked an experience, simulation, or activity in this book.

Culture crossers are part of a unique global, learning community. I happily immerse myself in education and surround myself with educators whose daily practice includes: 1) A desire to constantly improve upon their craft. 2) Keeping children at the centerpiece of learning. 3) Recognizing that positive attitude, innovation, and passion for our work is inspirational to those we serve. 4) Assuming responsibility for the tremendous influence we have on our students and on our profession. Finally, if anything I have written needs clarification, you can contact me through teachlearn-lead.net and I will do my best to respond. I am happy to walk you through any of these activities and add any extra information you might seek. The themes in Windows and Mirrors are universal ones so keep watch over that candle and let your light shine!

REFERENCES

Addison-Jacobson, J. and Addison, J. (1995, April). Service-learning in middle school: The day from hell. Paper presented at the annual meeting of the American Educational Research Association.

Billig, S.H., (2002). Service-learning. National Association of Elementary School Principals, Research Roundup 19(1).
Dewey,J. (1916). Democracy and education. New York, NY: The Free Press.

Dweck, C. (2006). Mindset: The New Psychology of Success.

Graessler, A.C., Moonjee,J., Duffy,D., (2008). Agent technologies designed to facilitate interactive knowledge construction. Discourse Processes, 45(4-5).

Halavais, A. (2008). Search engine society: digital media and society series. Cambridge: Polity.

Halsted, A. L., (1997). A bridge to adulthood: Service-learning at the middle level. Midpoints, 7(1), 3-13.

Harris, R. J. (2009). A Cognitive Psychology of Mass Communication, Fourth Edition (4th ed.). LEA.

Jonassen, David H. (2012). Meaningful learning with technology. 4th ed. Upper Saddle River, N.J.: Pearson/Merrill Prentice Hall.

Lysgaard, S. (1955). Adjustment in a Foreign Society: Norwegian Fulbright Grantees Visiting the United States.
International Social Science Bulletin, 7, 45-51.

Malone, T.W., (1981) Toward a theory of intrinsically motivating instruction, Cognitive Science, 4, 333-370.

Maslow, A. H. (1943). A theory of human motivation, Psychological Review 50, 370-96.

REFERENCES

Mezirow, Jack. (1978). Perspective transformation. Adult Education 28, 100-110.

Mezirow, Jack. (1991). Transformative dimensions of adult learning. San Francisco, CA: Jossey-Bass.

November, A. C. (2008). Web literacy for educators. Thousand Oaks, CA: Corwin Press.

Schrier, K., (2009). Using augmented reality games to teach 21st century skills.

Solomon, G. & Schrum, L. (2007). Web 2.0 New Tools, New Schools.

Steele, C. M. (1997). A threat in the air: How stereotypes shape intellectual identity and performance. American Psychologist, 52(6), 613-629

Tajfel, H. (1969), Cognitive Aspects of Prejudice. Journal of Social Issues, 25: 79–97.

Trepte, S. & Krämer, N. (2006). Expanding Social Identity Theory for Research in Media Effects: Two International Studies and a Theoretical Model. Paper presented at the annual meeting of the International Communication Association, Dresden International Congress Centre, Dresden, Germany

United Nations Sustainable Development Goals, www.UN.org

Walton, G. M., & Cohen, G. L. (2003). Stereotype lift. Journal of Experimental Social Psychology, 39(5), 456-467.

Wills, T. A. (1981). Downward comparison principles in social psychology. Psychological Bulletin, 90(2), 245-271.

Wiske, Martha Stone et al. (2005). Teaching for Understanding with Technology. San Francisco: Jossey-Bass.

ABOUT THE AUTHOR

Don't ask what the world needs. Ask what makes you come alive and go do it...for what the world needs are people who have come alive.

HOWARD THURMAN

A passionate edupreneur, school leader, and prolific author, Dean was recently appointed lead delegate for the inaugural 2023 GSEP Colloquium on youth social entrepreneurship in Hong Kong. He is a recipient of prestigious fellowships from EE Ford, the National Endowment of the Humanities, and the Klingenstein Foundation at Columbia University. He is an exemplar of a ravenous growth mindset earning a Masters in Education from Columbia University, a Masters in Teaching from the SIT Graduate Institute, a Proactive Leadership Certification from Cornell University, and a two-time selection in Harvard Graduate School of Education programs including "Redesigning American High Schools." To date, he has authored six books, published essays and briefs, and has appeared on over 25 expert panels and national podcasts.

His passion for developing youth leaders and building bridges of understanding between cultures has taken many forms including the founding of the Dominican Republic Orphanage project, the Center for Global Youth Leadership, and TLL Global. He service on boards and ambassadorial roles includes the Council for International Visitors, NAIS Global Ambassadorship, TABS-

NABI, and delegate to St. Lucia for the World Chamber of Commerce. In his career, he has established over 50 unique international partnerships, agreements, and exchanges with schools and businesses in China, Vietnam, Korea, Dominican Republic, Spain, Serbia, Bermuda, Colombia, Côte d'Ivoire, and more.

Currently, Dean serves as the Executive Head of School for two historic campuses in New York City, and his career as an educational leader has included decades in boarding schools and PK3-8 day schools throughout New York, New England and the southeast. In 2014, he founded the www.teachlearnlead.net professional development edu-library and built a globally engaged audience who utilize the vast curated resources. He credits his parents with instilling in him a love for social entrepreneurialism, service, community partnerships and civic impact. In their honor, he founded the Therese A. Fusto Micro-Grants to provide philanthropic seed money to promote youth leadership development of social and community impact projects.

www.ingramcontent.com/pod-product-compliance
Lightning Source LLC
Chambersburg PA
CBHW071236020426
42333CB00015B/1493